The Soul of Jerusalem

THE Soul OF Jerusalem

TEACHINGS OF
Rabbi Shlomo Carlebach

COMPILED BY RABBI SHLOMO KATZ

MOSAICA PRESS

Mosaica Press, Inc.

© 2014 by Mosaica Press

Edited by Doron Kornbluth

Typeset and designed by Rayzel Broyde

All rights reserved

ISBN 13: 978-1-937887-30-8   ISBN-10: 1937887308

No part of this publication may be translated, reproduced, stored in a retrieval system or transmitted in any form or by any means, electronic, mechanical, photocopying, recording, or otherwise, without prior permission in writing from both the copyright holder and the publisher.

Published and distributed by:

Mosaica Press, Inc.

www.mosaicapress.com

info@mosaicapress.com

ALSO BY RABBI SHLOMO KATZ: THE SOUL OF CHANUKA

All Jewish hearts beat to the pulse of Yerushalayim and every Jewish *neshamah* longs for our holy Temple to be rebuilt in all of its splendor.

May the words of Torah found herein help to shake the heavens and bring all Yidden closer to Hashem.

"If I forget you, O Jerusalem,

let my right hand forget it's skill".

B'simchah,

MICHAEL, LISA, ADAM AND DANIELLE WACHS

BS"D

In the merit of the speedy and full recovery of
our holy brother

Chiskiyahu Moshe Yaacov ben Mariasa

May Hashem bless him to receive all of our prayers and
love and may the power of our collective outpouring
open the gates for his healing.

With our deepest love, prayers, and blessings from
inside the holy walls of the Old City of Jerusalem,

ABA AND PAMELA CLAMAN

This holy *sefer* is dedicated

To all those fighting for the redemption of the "body" of the Land of Israel.

To all those preserving the "soul" of Am Yisrael and the Holy Land.

To those desperately trying to unite the "body" and "soul" of the Nation of Israel in the Holy Land.

To all those who were not privileged in their lifetime to see the Great Day — the 6 million, who opened the gates for us to come back to Eretz Yisrael.

To the holy soldiers who gave their lives fighting for the Holy Land.

To all the *korbanot tzibbur* who were killed in the various acts of Arab terror.

אורך ימים אשביעהו ואראהו בישועתי

To our holy rebbe Reb Shlomo zt"l, who gave us the vision of true freedom and redemption. Who taught us to sing and dance through the "night" and whose songs, stories, and holy teachings give us the strength to hold out until the Great Shabbos when the whole world will be one. Let it be soon! Let it be today!

Our prayer is that this holy sefer hasten the Great Day and arouse within us the deep longing and yearning for Yerushalayim and the Third Temple, for the unity of the Two Messiahs — Mashiach ben Yosef and Mashiach ben David — and for the unity of Yerushalayim shel Ma'alah and Yerushalayim shel Matah.

מצפים לישועה

באהבת עם ישראל וארץ ישראל

SIMCHA AND LEAH HOCHBAUM
CHEVRON, ISRAEL

In loving memory of

Dr. Leonard Sacharow,

whose love for children was boundless

TZILA SACHAROW

❧

Blessing all of Am Yisrael to hear Hashem's special melodies of Eretz Yisrael.

Much love, from my soul to yours, a fascinating part of Hashem's Creation.

ANONYMOUS

❧

To our holiest brother

Shlomo Katz

May Hashem continue to give you the strength to spread Torah from Jerusalem to the rest of the world.

We look forward to singing, dancing, learning, and praying with the entire *chevrah* in Jerusalem very soon.

With Much Love,

THE MOSTS AND THE COHENS

The Soul of Jerusalem

Contents

Preface	13
Acknowledgments	15
Chapter 1: The Temple	19
Chapter 2: Feeling the Pain of Destruction	43
Chapter 3: Missing Something When it's Already There	75
Chapter 4: G-d Never Left	82
Chapter 5: The Heart of Jerusalem	95
Chapter 6: The Holiness of Connection	142
Chapter 7: Seeing with G-d's Eyes	152
Chapter 8: What I Learn on Tisha b'Av	164
Chapter 9: The Third Temple	175
Appendix of Historical Personalities	204
About Rabbi Shlomo Carlebach	206
About the Author	208

Preface

"Rabbi, what are you most trying to connect your audience to?" the interviewer would often ask.

"By me, there are only two things, Yerushalayim and Shabbos. If I can connect people's souls to the depths of the Holy City, Yerushalayim, and to the holiness of Shabbos, that's all they really need in order to make it in This World."

Listening to Reb Shlomo zt"l teach about the Holy Temple and about the glory of Yerushalayim is an incredibly awesome experience. Transcribing those words is even deeper, but learning them takes it all to a higher, more exalted level. However, crying over Yerushalayim tops it all.

Still, what kind of crying are we talking about?

The Gemara says *Kol hamis'abel al Yerushalayim, zoche vero'eh besimchasah*" — "One who mourns over Jerusalem, will be privileged to see its rebuilding."[1] As Reb Shlomo zt"l taught, according to the Chassidic masters, the Talmud doesn't say that someday we will see the rebuilding.

It says that *while you are crying* you will see the rebuilding. What kind of crying is the Gemara talking about? The thing is like this. If you cry with anger, then nothing happens. But if you cry with longing, while you are crying — you are already there.

---

1   Tractate *Ta'anis* 30b

For the past number of years, we have spent many nights crying over these teachings. But together with our wonderful *chevreh* of students, the crying has been redirected and focused.

One of the hardest things for anyone to go through is to see their own father or mother crying. It's a very difficult and delicate thing to experience, regardless of your current status of relationship with your parents. It doesn't matter if it's a love/love, love/hate or G-d forbid a hate/hate relationship. When you see your parent in pain, something happens to you, something you wish you could ignore but you simply can't. It touches on the innermost private chamber of your being.

Crying over Yerushalayim has to do with my own sense of feeling homeless in this world. Longing for Yerushalayim to be rebuilt it's when I get a glimpse of G-d's pain. Once this happens, my own tears over seeing my Father cry rebuild me. They will also, essentially, rebuild my Father's broken home.

Rabbi Shlomo Carlebach *zt"l* (1925–1994) was a very rare and unique soul. A soul with a very rich and tight connection to his roots, but with an unprecedented way of seeing tomorrow.

With this unique vision in hand we welcome you to *The Soul of Jerusalem*, where one understands what they are missing on Tisha b'Av, but, at the same moment, begins to taste what G-d has been dreaming about from the Creation of the World — an eternal resting place for His Divine Presence.

Acknowledgments

Thank you, Master of the World, for giving me the undeserving privilege to work on this book. It has been a dream of mine for many years, and You sent me such an incredible world of family and friends for the journey.

To the Carlebach family: Neila, Neshama, Dari, and Ari. Everyone knows that every word that is in this *sefer* is a dream that your father had for you and your children. May all the dreams in this *sefer* come true in our own days, through our own days. May we be blessed to continue this holy work for the rest of our lives.

Tzlotana Midlo, your passion and dedication which you have blessed me to witness has taught me something which I pray will last forever. May you be blessed to have many more years of good health, and to continue bringing these holy teachings to the honorable place where they belong.

To Michael and Lisa Wachs, and your precious *kinderlach*, Adam and Danielle, thank you for being believers in this dream, and for being true teachers of perseverance in our lives.

Thank you Pamela and Aba Claman for the continuous love and support, giving so much strength to Am Yisrael, and specifically for all you do to help spread Reb Shlomo's message of oneness to the entire world.

To my dear friends Rav Simcha and Leah Hochbaum. Your encouragement and support (on all levels) constantly remind me how crucial it is not only to learn these teachings, but to live them as well.

To my dear friends Michael and Rivkah Most and Moshe and Aleezah Cohen. Having you in our lives brings us so much more meaning and gratitude to Hashem. Thank you for being a part of this incredible journey.

Nachman and Miriam Futterman, thank you for all your love, support, and hard work to enable the outpouring of our Rebbe's Torah in the world. I can't do any of this without you.

Alon Teeger, every teaching and story you have shared with me resonates so deep inside, and ignites me with so much strength to share these teachings with the world. To Nechama Silver, Arye Leib Weinger, and the rest of the board of the Rabbi Shlomo Carlebach Foundation, thank you for all your hard work and for making sure the vessel remains open.

Emuna Witt-Halevi, the gate we are all walking through was opened by you. To my old friend Shmalie Witt, you have such a big *cheilek* in all of this. Rabbi Eliezer and Rebbetzin Michele Garner, Rabbi Amihai Zippor, Netzach Sapir, Binyamin Miller, and Zusha Frumin, thank you for your monumental contributions to this publication. Thank you to *yedid nafshi* R' Judah and Ora Mischel, Yakir and Jackie Hyman, Tzila Sacharow, Michael and Miriam Perl, and Eden Pearlstein for all your encouragement, support, prayers, and help.

Sourcing this material was a project of its own, and there are many who helped with this task. Menachem Kallush, Rabbi Chaim Kramer, Rav Shaul Judelman, Rav Yitzchak Blau, Rav Raz Hartman, Rav Yehoshua Hartman, Yoel Petashnik, Reb Leibush Hundert, Yehudis Golshevsky, and Reb Moshe Stephansky, thank you so much for your help.

Thank you to Yeshivat Simchat Shlomo, headed by my dear friends Rav Sholom and Judy Brodt. We were privileged to learn many of these teachings in the Yeshiva. May you and the whole YSS family experience joy in the precious learning, and continue to bring *nachas* to all the tzaddikim.

To the wonderful and dedicated staff of Mosaica Press. Special thanks to Rav Yaacov Haber and Rabbi Doron Kornbluth: thank you for the *mesirus nefesh* in making sure we share this with the world.

My dear parents and siblings continue to be my strongest pillars of support. Your love for me and belief in this work are more than I could have ever asked for.

Lastly: to my Bina and our precious girls, who have truly taught me how to long for something once you already have it.

May our children see the fruits of our tears.

Shlomo Katz

Efrat, 5774

The Temple

The world usually translates the first word of the Torah as "In the beginning."

Bereishis does not mean "In the beginning."

The Medrash[2] says that *Bereishis* means "Because of the beginning." G-d created the world because of those people who know the secret of beginning.

Some people only know the secret of the end. For them, the world was a waste of time. Just suffering. Just survival.

The Medrash teaches us what is called a beginning: Israel is called a beginning; the Beis Hamikdash is called a beginning; Abraham is called a beginning.

The world is called a beginning. Do you know why the world is called a beginning? The whole world is always beginning.

Imagine if, G-d forbid, someone is going to commit suicide. You know what you do? You take a walk in the forest, not in the middle of the market. You go out to the forest where the world is the way G-d created it. What do you feel?

You feel like beginning all over again. Why so?

Because G-d created the world with beginnings, and the whole world is filled with beginnings.

Medrash Rabba Bereishis 1:4; Medrash Rabba Vayikra 36:4

Imagine that I'm overwhelmed and sad and I don't know what to do — I open the window to get myself some fresh air. What does air do to me? Fresh air gives me the strength to begin again.

Why is Yerushalayim so holy? Yerushalayim is so holy because if you just remember Yerushalayim, it gives you strength to begin.

What happened in the Holy Temple when people visited it?

Here comes a sinner, all his life he has sinned; everything is wrong. His soul is bankrupt. He walks into the Holy Temple — he walks out dancing. What happened to him? He has the strength to start. It's a new beginning.

We leave the Holy Temple different from the way we entered it.

How do we enter Yerushalayim?

How do we enter the Holy Temple?

Do you know what it means to purify yourself and come to the Holy Temple? It doesn't mean you leave your baggage outside and then you go in.

To come to the Holy Temple means you'll be standing before G-d. To stand before G-d means you have to take all your baggage in with you.

Imagine you have to see the President. You can't walk into his office with all your furniture, or even with a shopping bag. You leave everything outside. But when it comes to G-d, unless you come with everything, you're still not completely standing before Him. If you left something outside, only part of you is with Him — you're not fully with Him.

On Friday night, at the end of Lecha Dodi, we say "Bo'ee b'shalom," — "Come in peace the Sabbath Queen," and we turn around and look behind us.

What are we looking for? We look around to see if there is anything we might have forgotten to bring into Shabbos with us.

Some people say that in order to really be "in Shabbos," we have to leave all our baggage outside and be a little bit *Shabbosdik* for a day.

This is not real. *Mamesh* being "in Shabbos" means that we take everything we have and bring it with us into the Holy Day.

When we go for a walk, we don't turn around to see if we forgot anything, because we don't take everything with us for a little walk.

But when we move to a new place, we go back and make sure that we took everything. You're not supposed to walk into Shabbos — we are supposed to *move* into Shabbos. And if we really move into Shabbos, then before we enter we turn around and say, *"Bo'ee b'shalom"*, Come in peace. And right then we turn around to see if there is anything we forgot to bring into Shabbos with us.

We are supposed to come into Shabbos with everything we have. This is how a *Yiddele* walks into the Beis Hamikdash.

There is a little land. In that little land, there is a little city.

In that city there is a little street, and in that street there is a little wall.

When you stand by that Holy Wall, you can hear the footsteps of our father Abraham, and you can hear the trumpet of the Great Day to come. You hear the past and you can hear the future.

You can hear the singing of the Levites. Or, you can hear us crying, going into exile.

You can hear the 6 million crying out of the gas chambers, and you can hear the *Yiddelach's* tears in Siberia.

You can only see clearly if your eyes are filled with tears. When you stand by the Holy Wall and your tears are flowing, you see 6 million tears by that Holy Wall. You see the tears of Abraham, Isaac, and Jacob. You see the tears of King David. You can see the tears of your own children; you can see the tears of the whole world. You can hear people singing, singing the songs of yesterday, of tomorrow, of the Great Day to come.

The holiest time of the day is between day and night, when it's not night and it's not yet morning. Night doesn't want to leave the

Holy Wall, and the day doesn't want to drive out the night. They make peace between each other by that Holy Wall and they say, "let's be together, day and night, night and day." This is the holiest time by the Wall.

I was standing one early morning between day and night by the Holy Wall, and I was saying Kaddish for my father. But when you stand by that Holy Wall, you say Kaddish for the whole world. Sometimes you feel like saying Kaddish for your own soul, and sometimes you feel like saying Kaddish for tomorrow.

Then you hear the words "*Yisgadal V'yiskadash Shmei Raba*," — "May G-d's Name become great and sanctified," and you remember there is one G-d, and you know that the Great Morning is coming. You know that day and night will get together. The living and the dead, we and the whole world.

This is my song, the song of tears, because on that Great Day the tears will march through the world, and the whole world will join them. The tears will clear the world and prepare the world. Everything will come together. We will all come together. It will be a new morning. A new beginning.

The first line of the Torah says, "*Bereishis bara Elokim es hashamayim v'es ha'aretz*" — "In the beginning G-d created heaven and earth." And the verse continues, "*V'ha'aretz haysa sohu vavohu*," — "And the land was in chaos;" "*v'Ruach Elokim merachefes al pnei hamayim*" — "And the Spirit of G-d was upon the waters."[3]

The Medrash asks, "What was the Spirit of G-d which was upon the waters?"

The Spirit of G-d refers to *rucho shel* Mashiach, the spirit of Mashiach.

---

3 Bereishis 1:1-2

Then it says "*Vayomer Elokim yehi ohr*"[4] — "G-d said, 'Let there be light'" — "*va'yehi ohr*" — "and there was light." That means that someday, when Mashiach comes, it will be the time for G-d to say, "Let there be light."

Now listen to this. "'*V'ha'aretz*,"—"and the land" — this is the Holy Land. What other land could the Torah be talking about?

"*V'ha'aretz haysa sohu vavohu*," the land was *mamesh* in chaos — this is the *churban* Beis Hamikdash.

"*v'Ruach Elokim merachefes al pnei hamayim*" — "And the Spirit of G-d was upon the waters."

The Medrash asks: "What were these waters?" And it answers, "These were all the tears that were shed over the destruction."

Who was crying over the destruction? The Jewish people were crying. G-d was crying.

In Hebrew, there is no singular term for water. *Mayim* is always plural. Since *mayim* can mean the tears, it's always two tears.

In other words, when I am crying, G-d is crying. There has never been one tear in the world. With every tear that someone sheds, G-d is crying also. Two tears, at least. Every time. No one has ever cried alone.

We know that the first two letters of the Hebrew alphabet are *alef* and *beis*. And the strangest thing is: "*Bereishis bara*," the phrase describing the creation of the world, begins with *beis*. And the Ten Commandments, the Torah, begin with *alef*.

What caused the destruction of the world? The *alef* and the *beis*, the physical world and the Torah, never got together.

It's the same thing for us in our personal lives. The conflict inside every human being is a conflict between the *alef* and the *beis*. Our *beis*, our physical world, has not been completely integrated into our *alef*, the Torah.

Or that some of our *alef*, our Torah, didn't get deep enough into our *kishkes*, our physical being. The *alef* and the *beis* just never got together — which results in destruction.

---

4   Bereishis 1:3

We try our best. We hang on a little bit, bouncing back and forth between the *alef* and the *beis*, clinging to both but without them being connected. We just aren't whole. We are not completely natural and not completely unnatural; we are a little bit good and a little bit evil — a little bit in the world, a little bit following our nature, a little bit connected to Yiddishkeit — everything a little bit.

This is chaos. Do you know what "*Sohu vavohu*" means? Chaos means that everything is there — but not in the right place.

Imagine that I come into your house and it's *mamesh* chaos. This doesn't mean there's no kitchen, no bathroom. Chaos means that the couch is on top of the stove. What's going on here? I mean, I know you need a couch and you need a stove, but not in the same place.

If you have a bed and table, it's beautiful. I'm glad you have a table and you have a bed. But will you please put it all in order? Otherwise it seems like total destruction, "*sohu vavohu.*"

Chaos. Everything is there, but not in the right place. It never came together.

You see what it is: It is possible for a couple to hang on to each other for 2,000 years, but they never really got together. Still, it's also not bad enough to divorce each other. It's not living, but it's also not dying. Then, something happens, and they just can't go on the way they are going now. So they separate. Do you know what happens then? Suddenly, after they separate, they realize that they really belonged to each other. You see, their staying together was not the cure — their cure was the separation.

The way things are now is no good. Too much chaos. Half here and half there.

Inside, we know that we cannot live with only the *alef* or the *beis*. Even if we have both, we need them together. So the world — and we in our own lives — start getting the *alef* and the *beis* back together again.

Do you know where this happened? Where did everything find its right place?

The Holy Temple. We went into the Temple with everything we

had. All our shame, fears, and guilt. We came out singing. How? What happened?

The Holy Temple put everything in its right place. In the Holy Temple, G-d brought the *alef* and *beis* together again. The Beis Hamikdash is where everything came together. The complete integration between the Torah and the World.

◈

Sometimes, I tell my child to close the door, and she doesn't want to do it. So then I say, "I want you to close the door!"

How close am I to my child at that moment? Not very. It is my wants against hers.

Now open your hearts wide.

Anything which has to do with "wanting" doesn't have closeness. There is no love going on, no real yearning.

If, G-d forbid, I am sick, my mind says to my foot "Do me a favor and move." But my foot doesn't move. Do you know why? My foot is not close to my mind. When they are close, everything happens automatically.

Do you know what happened in the Beis Hamikdash? Reb Nachman calls it *He'aras haratson*[5] the "enlightenment of will" — G-d's Will was shining into us so strongly that it was like my foot responding to my mind without any trouble.

It was not that G-d "wanted" me to do something or was trying to get me to do certain things. In the Holy Temple, what G-d wanted me to do was so real and so clear, that it filled me with light and such a longing that all my life should be according to G-d's Will. I was as connected to G-d as my foot is connected to my brain. Our beings were all together and all together with G-d.

In the Holy Temple, all our fears, doubts, arguments... they all faded away in the Oneness of G-d.

---

5   *Likutei Halachos*, Orach Chayim Hilchos Birkas Harei'ach

According to Kabbalah, the two most important letters in the Hebrew alphabet are *mem* and *samech*.[6] Moshe Rabbeinu gave us the Torah in 40 days — in *mem* days, because the numerical value of *mem* is 40. The form of *mem* at the end of a word is like a box. So *mem* surrounds you. Being like a box, the *mem* also has corners — and sometimes you can hurt yourself on a sharp corner.

But the *samech* — it's a whole different thing. The *samech* is round, with no corners. Aharon HaKohen is the master of the *samech*. "*Somech Hashem l'chol ha-noflim*" — "G-d is a support to all who are falling." *Samech* supports you. That's something else.

Moshe Rabbeinu begged G-d to give the Torah through Aharon. He argued with G-d for eight days, but G-d said no. What was Moshe really asking G-d? He wanted us to be given the Torah of the round, supportive *samech*, not the Torah of the *mem*, of the forty days. A different Torah.

The truth is that you need the Torah of the *mem*. Imagine if I tell my children, "I love you, and anything you do is okay with me." They'll say, "So mazel tov, I'll do anything in the world I want to do."

There has to be a *mem*. There has to be a sharpness of corners that tells us, "Listen, if you do this, it's wrong; and if you do that, it's right." The world has to know that killing is wrong, stealing is wrong, and other things are good. There has to be a *mem*, even if it hurts a little bit.

But after the *mem* comes the *samech*. You know friends, we've always had the Torah. We stood on Mount Sinai, we received the Torah, and we still have it. So what's our problem?

Our trouble is that when it comes to the Holy Temple in Jerusalem, the Beis Hamikdash, you need the *samech*. In fact, the Temple is the center for the *samech*. "*Yerushalayim harim saviv la*"[7] — "Jerusalem

---

6   Based on Tractate *Megillah* 3a
7   Tehillim 125:2

is surrounded by mountains." It is surrounded, cushioned, supported by the mountains. And Yerushalayim is the center. What's a *samech*? It is always round. A center doesn't have corners, so it can't hurt you. The center of our round *samech* is the Holy City of Jerusalem.

And this is our problem, this is what it means to be in exile. We know the Torah of the *mem*, but we don't know the Torah of the *samech* anymore…

In the Temple, we had the *mem* and the *samech*. We were directed, we knew G-d's Will. It was clear. That's the *mem*. And we were supported, surrounded, and loved. That's the *samech*.

Can you imagine what it felt like? Can you imagine being there for even one moment?

In the Holy Temple, the most important part was the singing — the singing of the holy tribe, the Levites.

According to our tradition, there were 50,000 instruments and 100,000 voices. They would alternate every few minutes, day and night. They would sing and play for the One, for the only One. Every note and every melody was the deepest prayer in the world. Those songs and prayers reached so deep, they reached into the deepest depths of every human being. You cannot hear those melodies and those prayers without returning to the One, to the only One.

Sadly enough, since the destruction of the Holy Temple, we do not sing these songs. "*Eich nashir es shir Hashem al admas neichar*,"[8] How could we sing these holy songs on unholy soil?

On the other hand, how can you live without those holy melodies?

How can a Jew live for one moment without hearing a song of the holy Levites?

Do you hear them late at night in your dreams?

Do you hear the Levites?

---

8   Tehillim 137:4

Do you hear the 100,000 voices and the 50,000 instruments?

I remember that, when I was a little boy, I would always ask my father and my mother, "Don't you remember one melody from the Holy Temple?"

But they didn't know any. I asked great rabbis to teach me one melody. But they couldn't.

I was desperate, just about to give up. Then one day I met an old Chassid from Russia who had spent ten years in Siberia. This person was ready to live and die for G-d a million times a second.

I asked him, "Don't you know at least one melody from the Beis Hamikdash?"

The Chassid smiled at me. He put his holy hand on my shoulder and said what I had been hoping for so many years to hear: "My dear young man, let me tell you. When I was young I met an old Chassid who told me something he heard from other Chassidim: according to the Ba'al Shem Tov, the way we chant the prayers of the High Holidays is a little bit, and maybe all of it, from the Holy Temple."

Do you know what this means? This means that in a way, we can still enter the Holy Temple today. The Levites are still singing.

In fact, the Holy Temple is still standing.

Let me explain.

Everyone thinks that the Holy Temple was destroyed. It's not true. Three times a day, when we pray, it's as if we are in the Holy Temple.

The first Holy Temple was built because of Avraham, who was the first one to pray the morning prayer. Sadly enough, it was destroyed.

The second Holy Temple was built because of Yitzchak and the afternoon prayer, but sadly enough it was also destroyed.

The third Temple will be built because of our holy father Ya'akov, and it can't be destroyed because our holy father Ya'akov initiated the evening prayer. Ya'akov Avinu opened our hearts even while we were in the lowest, darkest night. You can still hear him saying to every Jew who ever lived until Mashiach comes, "Don't give up, G-d is with you. You are always in Yerushalayim; you are always in the Holy Temple.

There is no power in the world that can destroy the Holy Temple. There is no power in the world that can estrange you from G-d."

What's the Holy Temple all about? The Temple is G-d's house. A house means permanence. You know friends, when I stay in a hotel, my feet are there, my hands are there and my head is there, but something is missing.

My heart is not in the hotel. My soul is not in the hotel.

My house is the place in which I am completely there. I can take a trip for five years and come back, but it's still my house. The house is the deepest connection I have.

When we made the golden calf, the problem was that we obviously weren't connected to G-d that strongly. We stood on Mount Sinai and received the Torah, but the connection was still not so good.

The Holy Temple is absolutely the most permanent connection. Why was the Holy Wall never destroyed? Because we never stopped being connected to it. Even though the other walls were still destroyed, there is something very deep inside of me that never left the Western Wall.

The Holy Temple is still standing.

The only question is for each of us — are we ready to enter it?

The way we look today, physically, mentally, spiritually; in every way… do you think we are supposed to look like the way we look today?

It's not a question of being free, being in the Holy Land or not. We are completely different people. Physically, before the destruction of the Temple, we were such beautiful people. There is a whole Medrash about how beautiful the children were in Jerusalem, the most beautiful children in the world.

Do you know how strong we were physically?

Who do you think was physically stronger — Ya'akov or Esav?

The truth is that Ya'akov Avinu was so much stronger than Esav.

It says "Ya'akov *ish tam*,"[9] Ya'akov was perfect — in everything there is in the world.

Can you imagine how beautiful Adam was? He was created by G-d, G-d created the most perfect person in the world. Does anybody know who looked exactly like Adam?

Ya'akov Avinu.

Who was the first woman who looked exactly like Eve before she was driven out of Paradise?

Sarah and Rachel, those two mothers.

When Rivkah was in the house of Lavan, she was beautiful but not that beautiful. The moment she entered the tent of Sarah, she looked exactly like Eve did before she was driven out of Paradise. So Sarah looked like the most beautiful woman in the world.

This is all just physically.

Spiritually, it was absolutely divine.

The Medrash[10] says that each person in Yerushalayim had eleven crowns on their head. We had the crown of Avraham, the crown of Yitzchak, the crown of Yosef, the crown of Moshe, the crown of the Torah, the crown of Priesthood, the crown of the Levites, the crown of prophecy, the crown of the Beis Hamikdash, the crown of all of Israel, and the crown of the Mashiach.

Unfortunately, it didn't last. Listen to the saddest thing in the world:

When the enemies took over, all those eleven crowns were taken from us. They think they own the crowns now, but in Tehillim it says "*V'chol karnei resha'im agade'a u'seromamena karnos tzaddik*". All the wicked people who think they are wearing the crown, G-d says "I will take it away from them and give it back to the highness of the tzaddik," the holy people.

When will he give it back to us? It says "*Veyiten oze l'malko veyarem keren meshicho*". Mashiach is coming; he will give it back to us.

---

9   Bereishis 25:27
10 Medrash Eichah 2:6

The Temple *was* beautiful and we were beautiful in it. And so it will be, again.

❧

The Gemara says "*Asara kabin yofi yardu la'olam*".[11] "Ten measures of beauty came down to the world," Yerushalayim took nine and one was for the rest of the world. Yerushalayim is very beautiful and the most beautiful place in Yerushalayim is the Holy Temple.

Reb Nachman says that the destruction of the Temple means that the beauty of the world is destroyed.[12] Today in the world, what is called beautiful? The more ugly, shallow, and stupid it is, the more the world thinks it's beautiful. Real beauty is meaningless in the world, only because the Holy Temple is destroyed.

What does it mean for me as a private person? Reb Nachman says something very strong. How does it sound to you if two people meet and the whole time they tell you how beautiful they are?

Imagine you'll meet a girl and she says, "Obviously, I'm the most beautiful girl in the world, I hope you are not nearsighted…"

You look at her, and each time she says how beautiful she is, she looks more ugly. Finally, after an hour of her saying how beautiful she is, you just can't stand it, and you take off fast.

Imagine if you meet someone and they tell you how beautiful someone else is. Each time they tell you something beautiful about someone else, they themselves get more beautiful — in a real and deep way.

❧

Two things in the world are called beauty, the Torah and the Beis Hamikdash.

---

11 Tractate *Kiddushin* 49b
12 *Likutei Moharan* 2:67

My body lives in a physical house.

Where does my soul live?

The Torah that I learn, the beauty emanating from the Torah which I'm thinking about, is where the soul lives. These are the four walls of my *neshamah*. If I'm filled with thinking of my own beauty, it's ugly. If I'm thinking the whole time how beautiful G-d is, how beautiful Yerushalayim is, how beautiful the world is, how beautiful the Torah is, it's a different kind of thing.

Imagine you meet someone and you just want to tell them so badly what a beautiful thing you just did. You are itching to tell them, but you control yourself and you don't.

Reb Nachman says that with this little strength you put in… this is the way to build the Beis Hamikdash. Each time you want to say something good about yourself and you hold back — it builds you and the whole world with you. After that, when you learn Torah, you'll understand it better because suddenly G-d opens the beauty of learning before you. Each time you want to say something beautiful about what you did, but you don't — G-d shows you the beauty of Israel and you are a little bit on your way to rebuild the Beis Hamikdash.

There is a *pasuk* that says "*Oz vesiferes b'mikdasho*".[13] You know what the hardest thing in the world is? I'm sure everyone has trouble with it. When we do something beautiful and I tell it to someone, so it's as if I got it out of my system, I really knocked it out of the inside of me. You vomit it out so it's not in your *kishkes* no more. If you can only hold back it stays inside and it is surrounding you, surrounding the inside of you.

So Reb Nachman says *oz*, takes a lot of strength, but *v'siferes*… that everything you do beautiful *b'mikdasho*, stays inside, in your holy compound. Don't say it.

---

13   Tehillim 96:6

There is a beautiful teaching of Reb Tzadok HaKohen: What makes one *Yiddele* more of a *Yiddele* than another *Yiddele*?

How come when one *Yiddele* talks to you, he *mamesh* wakes up your insides and you know what it is to be a *Yiddele*.

Another *Yiddele* talks to you and nothing happens to your insides.

It could even be that both *Yiddelach*, on the level of doing, are both doing the same thing. They work the same, eat the same… and maybe even pray the same.

The answer is that it doesn't depend on how much you're doing. The question is: While you are doing whatever it is that you are doing, how much are you aware that there is one G-d? How much is the light of G-d shining into you?

Being more of a *Yiddele* means that more of G-d is shining into you. Less of a *Yiddele* means… it's not shining so much.

The Holy Temple was the headquarters for G-d's shining in this world.

When I walked into the Holy Temple I might have been less of a *Yiddele*, but *gevalt* how much more of a *Yiddele* I would be when I walked out.

Reb Tzadok HaKohen teaches: There are three revelations of G-d, there is *ani*, there is *atah*, and there is *hu*. Sometimes, it's on the level of "*ani*", which is "I," sometimes on the level of "*atah*" which is "you," sometimes on the level of "*hu*" which is "Him."[14]

There is a *pasuk* that says, "Ani Hashem hashochen itam b'soch tum'asam."[15] G-d says, "I, G-d, am with them, even if they ignored the laws." It means that there is a little of Hashem in them, even if they get to the lowest place. That revelation of G-d in the lowest place is called *Ani*.

---

14   *Tzidkas Hatzaddik* 247
15   Vayikra 16:16

Then there is another revelation, which is called *Atah*. When I'm *mamesh* talking to G-d. I *mamesh* know He's there. I say *Baruch ata Hashem*.

Then there is the level of *Baruch Hu*, "*Baruch Hu Baruch Shmo*" or "*Asher kidishanu b'mitzvosav v'tzivanu.*" Both of these are on the level of *Hu*. I don't know where He is, it's beyond me, I cannot fathom.

Ani is obviously always there. "*Ani Hashem hashochen itam b'soch tum'asam,*" G-d is always there, even *chas v'shalom* in the lowest depths. That means He's always there... always, always, always there.

But obviously it's such a small revelation that you can sit there and steal and rob and kill and do everything wrong, and G-d is still there. It's the kind of revelation that doesn't disturb you.

The level of *Atah* is a very high level. *Mamesh* to be aware that G-d is right here. That is higher. Not just that He is here, but that I can't ignore Him! The *heilige* Reb Tzadok says that the Holiness of the Holy Land, of Eretz Yisrael, is on the level of *Atah*.

When it comes to the Holiness of Moshe Rabbeinu, Moshe Rabbeinu is on the level of *Hu*. Moshe Rabbeinu was so much aware of G-d that he realized that I don't know anything. It means I cannot address Him like He is *He*, I can only address Him like I don't know who He is. It's too much.

Then there was the Beis Hamikdash. What's the holiness of the Beis Hamikdash? The holiness of the Beis Hamikdash is something unbelievable. The *Atah* and the *Hu* meet together.

For the High Priest in the Holy of Holies, it was even more. It was not *Ani*, it wasn't *Atah*, it wasn't *Hu*. It was higher than all of this.

And here I want you to open your hearts in the deepest depths.

Everybody knows the Beis Hamikdash has two names. The Beis Hamikdash is called a Mishkan, and the Beis Hamikdash is called a Mikdash.

Mishkan means dwelling. The Mishkan is that kind of holiness which is on the level of *Ata*, when you *mamesh* see it.

Basically, when I do a mitzvah, I make a vessel for G-d. The moment you make a vessel for G-d, it's an indwelling, it's limited, it's right here. But the level which you yourself do is on the level of *Atah*. When I make a mitzvah I address G-d in the present. Like He is *mamesh* here, face-to-face. I say *Baruch Atah Hashem*, I'm doing a mitzvah, I'm putting on tefillin. I look at the tefillin and see G-d's light. I see His Will, I say *Baruch Atah*.

The holiness of a *Yiddele* is that it's not just the holiness of doing a mitzvah. There is a kind of holiness that is inside of me. I know it's there. I just can't put my finger on it.

And listen to this very deep thing. It's not that kind of holiness that I can say, G-d is within me even if I do wrong, on the level of *Ani*. It's not *Ani*.

There is something *so* holy inside of me, absolutely untouched. You cannot address it face-to-face, it doesn't show anywhere, and it's there.

Every moment that you shine into your heart that there is *mamesh* one G-d, all the darkness is expelled from your heart. All the darkness inside of us is only because it's not completely filled with that knowledge that there really is one G-d.

I believe in G-d. Our knowledge of G-d, is on the level of *Ani*. Sometimes, we can get to the *Atah*. Rarely, very rarely, we get to the *Hu*.

In the Temple, we connected to G-d in all three. In the Temple, G-d's presence was real, *mamesh* immediate, and full of Awe — way beyond.

That's the Mishkan. That's the Beis Hamikdash. That's Yerushalayim.

※

In the Temple, we could connect to G-d on levels we can't even understand. Directly. Indirectly. When we felt low, when we felt high. In ways that we can't even imagine.

The Temple was lost, but wasn't really lost.

Do you know what it means that the Holy Temple was destroyed? Open your hearts in the deepest depths.

If I love you very much, whenever I communicate with you, I want us to be hidden. I want to be alone with you somewhere.

As long as we had the Beis Hamikdash, we were so close to the One, to the only One. The Holy Temple was a house of prayer where we could talk privately to G-d. But now we are a little far away, and there is no longer a Temple, a house of prayer. And even in our synagogues, all of us feel how our prayers are still destroyed.

The most beautiful thing is happening in the world today. There is such a need, such a longing, such a crying for the Holy Temple. We want to be so close to G-d again; we want to be so close to each other. Husband and wife want to be so close; parents and children, friends, and people all over the world are hearing the words of the prophet who says, "So says G-d: The Beis Hamikdash is a house of prayer for everyone, like it is written: '*Ki beisi beis tefillah yikare l'chol ha'amim* — My house is a house of prayer for all nations'."[16]

We want the closeness to G-d. We want the oneness and aloneness with G-d.

We can have it friends, we can *mamesh* have it.

The first time I was in Jerusalem was in 1959, and my last night there was such a *gevalt* because I didn't know when I'd be back. I was walking around the city with some of the *chevreh* and the whole time I was thinking: *I wonder how many times I've been in this world during the last 2,000 years of exile.*

But of one thing I was certain — that all of us were there when we were driven out of Yerushalayim.

We were all there.

---

16   Yishayahu 56:7

We can still feel it today when we have to leave Jerusalem; we can feel our hands and feet chained, walking down.

And then I thought — despite the Romans and their hatred, I'm sure the Yidden were singing, even as they went into exile. And suddenly this *niggun* came into my head:

"*Le'olam lo eshkach pikudecha ki vam chiyisani*" —"I will never forget Your teachings because they are my life."[17]

There is a Medrash that asks: "Have you ever heard of a person who forgot to breathe? Never — because our lives depend on our breathing."

In the same way, we can't forget G-d's teachings, because they are our life. And even more so, we can never forget Yerushalayim, because our lives *mamesh* depend on the Holy City....

Lets's ask ourselves one of the most difficult questions in the world. Do we want the Beis Hamikdash? The way I live, do I really need the Beis Hamikdash?

And sadly enough, I have to answer that the way I live, I don't really feel that I need the Holy Temple. *Gevalt*, how far we are from Yiddishkeit! And I'm not even talking now about not being the way we're supposed to be. I can do everything right; I can keep Shabbos, put on tefillin, learn Torah.

But I really don't feel I need the Beis Hamikdash, *chas v'shalom*.

Our holy forefathers — Avraham, Yitzhak, Ya'akov, Yosef, and the holy tribes — everything in their lives had to do with the Beis Hamikdash — everything in the world.

Without going into the depths: Ya'akov met Rachel, and he kissed her. And he began to cry.[18] Why was he crying? Because he saw the destruction of the Temple, and he saw that, because of the destruction,

---

17   Tehillim 119:93
18   Bereishis 29:11

Rachel would not be buried next to him. He *mamesh* saw the whole thing.

And when it comes to Yosef — when Yosef met his brothers he said: "I'm Yosef, your brother." He cried on Binyamin's shoulder, and Binyamin cried on his. What were they crying about? Binyamin was crying for the Mishkan, the Tabernacle that stood in his part of Israel, and Yosef was crying for the Holy Temple.[19]

Everything was about the Beis Hamikdash. The Holy Temple was the center of their lives.

I don't think my father could talk to me for more than 15 minutes without mentioning the Beis Hamikdash. He could have been talking about anything, but one way or the other, without his even knowing it, everything had to do with the Beis Hamikdash and Yerushalayim. And my father told me that the words Yerushalayim and Beis Hamikdash were on my Zeide's tongue all the time.

We need to give this over to our children. Our children should *mamesh* live in a world which already has a Holy Temple. We should always have the word "Beis Hamikdash" on our tongues.

Sometimes we are angry at G-d because we think that He doesn't listen to our prayers. Reb Tzadok HaKohen says something so strong.[20] The truth is that G-d listens to every prayer. But sometimes, while I am praying, I'm already making plans of what to do if G-d doesn't help me.

So G-d says, "Listen, brother, do your thing. I don't want to disturb your plans."

Imagine what would happen if a *Yiddele* came to G-d and said, "Ribbono Shel Olam, I *mamesh* don't know what to do." We still think we could manage without the Beis Hamikdash, without the Holy

---

19   Bereishis 45:14, *Rashi*
20   *Tzidkas Hatzaddik* 211, 212, 213

Temple. We still think we can manage without Mashiach's coming. Let's be very honest with each other. We all are hoping for Mashiach to come, but we are still making plans in case he doesn't...

Sometimes I look at my little daughter, and I want nothing more than for Mashiach to be here to teach her. But then I think that if the Messiah doesn't come, I might send her to this school or to that school.

The Ribbono Shel Olam says, "Listen, brother, don't let me interfere with your daughter's education. Do your thing." But imagine what would happen if I stood before G-d and said, "Ribbono Shel Olam, I *mamesh* need the Mashiach because I have nobody else to send my daughter to study with." Then the Messiah would *mamesh* be here.

There is a passage in Psalms, and this is what it says. "*Even ma'asu habonim haysa l'rosh pinah*" — "The stone which was cast away by the builders," the stone which was a misfit, "became the crown of building."[21]

One of the rules of the building of the Holy Temple was that you couldn't cut. You couldn't cut stones, you couldn't cut anything.

Sometimes I wish I could teach parents how not to cut down their children. Children are so holy, they are little Holy Temples. They are little holy stones in the Beis Hamikdash. You can't build a Holy Temple with cut up stones. If you ever stand by the Holy Wall, it's the strangest sight in the world. One stone is big, one stone is small. One had four corners, one has eight corners. But the great miracle is that they all fit together.

So when the people were building the Beis Hamikdash, they used uncut stones, and it all went very well. But there was one stone which was an absolute misfit, so the builders threw that stone away. Then

---

21   Tehillim 118:22

they started building the Holy of Holiest, and the Holy of Holiest had a little roof. There was an opening in the roof, a strange kind of opening, and there was no stone which fit that opening. Suddenly, the builders remembered the misfit, the stone which was cast away. It was the only stone which fit the opening, the only stone which could be the crown on the building.

King David asked why this was so. And he answered *"Me'eis Hashem haysa zos hee nifla'as b'eineinu"*[22] — because it's G-d world, because G-d is working wonders. Only a real misfit, only someone who has been cast away by the world, can be the crown of G-d's building.

All the young people of the world today, all the holy beggars, are also so-called misfits. But on the great day when Mashiach comes, they will be the crown of the world. Believe me, the Messiah will not surround himself with anybody else — only with castaway stones. Only with those holy castaway stones. Do you know why? Because *"Me'eis Hashem haysa zos"* — it's G-d's world.

There are two types of crying. There is crying from anger, and there is a crying of longing. On Tisha b'Av the crying is from longing, because on Tisha b'Av I feel again how beautiful the Beis Hamikdash was, and how much I wish it was still there.

The Gemara says *"Kol hamis'abel al Yerushalayim, zoche v'ro'eh besimchasah"* — "If you are mourning over Jerusalem, you will be privileged to see the rebuilding."[23]

According to the Chassidishe Rebbes, the Talmud doesn't say that someday we will see the rebuilding. It says that *while you are crying* you will see the rebuilding. What kind of crying is the Gemara talking about?

The thing is like this. If you cry with anger, then nothing happens. But if you cry with longing, while you are crying, you are already there.

---

22   Tehillim 118:23
23   Tractate *Ta'anis* 8:23k 30b

Basically, a person is capable of wanting two different things in two different ways at the very same time. Imagine I'm very tired and I really want to sleep. But I know I have to get up, so I also want that. What's the difference between my wanting to continue to sleep and my wanting to get up? I want to get up because I have to. That's a really bad scene, because I'm not longing for it. But I really want to sleep — I'm *mamesh* longing to sleep.

To be in exile means that whatever I do is because I have to. To be free, to be redeemed, means that whatever I want to do is what I am longing to do.

So you see, in the Beis Hamikdash, all the wanting was on the level of longing. Whatever we wanted to do was for real. After the destruction of the Temple we went into exile, so all the wanting in the world is now on the level of "I have to."

Now open your hearts.

A person who never really loved someone else enough to miss them *mamesh* doesn't know what love is. I'm sure it's clear to you that the depths of loving is not what you feel when you are with the person. Real loving is the missing...

Now imagine I love somebody very much and then, somehow, we part from each other. So I really miss this person. Then, after we've been apart for a while, I suddenly think: *Could it be, am I already so far from you that I don't even miss you anymore? Oy vey, we have got to get it together.*

So often we hear people say not only do they want to be holy, they want to want to be holy.

This is the thing about Tisha b'Av. On Tisha b'Av it becomes clear to me that I have forgotten how to long for something. I long to long again. And I also realize that I'm so far away from the Beis Hamikdash that I don't even know what I have lost. I don't really miss it anymore. And *gevalt*, do I miss that missing.

This missing of the missing is absolutely the deepest depths in the world.

The Holy Maharal said that the night is so holy, that it is not part of time and is not part of space.[24] Night people know that no time and no space could keep souls apart from each other.

Late at night, when you think of the Beis Hamikdash, you are right there in the Temple. When we think of a friend late at night, you are right with them, and late at night, if we think of Shabbos, of the Great Shabbos, we can taste the Great Dawn.

ص

We *Yiddelach* are connected to two levels of holiness. There is *kodesh*, holy, and there is *Kodesh Kodashim*, holy of holies.

When you walk away from the Holy Wall, you may still not keep Shabbos and you may not be able to handle Yom Kippur. So maybe you're not holy yet. But do you know what you are connecting to at the Holy Wall? Your Holy of Holies.

And do you know why the Holy Temple was destroyed? Because the Yidden hated each other. To hate somebody is just an ordinary sin like not eating kosher, like not putting on tefillin. On the level of holiness, it's just another sin, even a minor one. But on the level of Holy of Holies, if you hate somebody you can't go into the Holy Temple. On the level of Holy of Holies, hatred is not only a sin — it just can't be. There is absolutely no room for hatred in the Holy of Holies.

When Mashiach comes, he will turn the whole world on to G-d. Why haven't we done that already? We have the Torah. Isn't it very holy? Yes, but it is not the Holy of Holies.

The Holy of Holies is Yerushalayim. The Holy of Holies is the Holy Temple. So we can't turn the whole world on to G-d until Yerushalayim and the Beis Hamikdash are built again.

---

24 *Nesiv Hatorah*, Chapters 4, 9

2
Feeling the Pain of Destruction

Tisha b'Av is the day of the destruction of the Temple. The strangest thing in the world is that there is no house in the world that is so completely rebuilt like the destroyed Temple. It's there, in such a strong way. But it also isn't there.

Now, here, open your hearts. If you love someone very much and you don't see them, you miss them very much.

If you come to the place that you always met, let's say, you always met under a certain tree, and you come there to that tree, and the person you love is not there… it is so hard, much harder… they are gone, but in a way, they are still there.

We know that the Holy Temple is destroyed. The feeling is strongest when you stand by the Holy Wall, because there you miss the Temple so much. G-d took us back to Jerusalem, and G-d took us back to the Holy Wall because He really believed that very soon — maybe today, maybe tomorrow — G-d will rebuild the world again and rebuild the Holy Temple.

We have to be there, we can't just miss the Holy Temple from afar. We have to be there. You have to stand by the Holy Wall and miss the Holy Temple, miss the wholeness of the world, miss the wholeness of your own soul.

It's all the same. The Holy Temple is just a little mirror of the world.

When the Holy Temple is whole, the whole world is whole.

When the Holy Temple is destroyed, the whole world is destroyed.

Do you know what the greatness of our generation is? At least we can put our finger on it. We know what's wrong with the world. We are standing right by the broken down vessels and saying "This has to be corrected."

We are standing by the Holy Wall in Yerushalayim and saying, "G-d, what can we do? What can You do?"

This Tisha b'Av should wake up everything holy inside of us which we didn't even know about. Today, we know that we are only using maybe five or ten percent of our brain. Imagine how little we use of our holiness. Even less. Maybe almost none at all.

On Tisha b'Av, we are not only crying over the destruction of the Temple, we are crying over the destruction of every Yid. Exile destroyed us, much more than it destroyed a building. Exile took the best of our kids, the biggest *neshamahs*, the sweetest. They can't find the Beis Hamikdash, they can't find the Holy Temple in Jerusalem — or in themselves.

The more you understand the destruction of Yerushalayim, the more you understand your own destruction.

In 1963, I had the privilege of being with the Holy Vizhnitzer Rebbe in St. Moritz, Switzerland on Tisha b'Av. And there was a *Yiddele* there who started chanting Eichah, (the Book of Lamentations) but he was crying so much that he made the reading very long.

So the Vizhnitzer said, "Please make it fast". The *Yiddele* didn't make it fast, so the Rebbe gave Eichah to somebody else to read.

At the end of Eichah, everybody was standing around the Holy Vizhnitzer. And the Rebbe said, "I want you to know, my holy father, the *heilige* Reb Yisrael Vizhnitzer, was up all night on Tisha b'Av. And he had some Yidden with him who knew some *niggunim*, some melodies, which were not so sad and not really happy but were in-between —

they were holy *niggunim* for Eichah. My father and his Chassidim were up all night singing Eichah — but not with the traditional melody, with other *niggunim*."

I didn't understand why the Rebbe told us this until I found a mind-blowing teaching by the Radomsker Rebbe. He said like this:

"When a son is crying, a good father consoles his son. What happens when both the father and the son are crying? If the son is a good son, then for a few moments he forgets his own pain and tries to console his father."

On Tisha b'Av, we are sad because of what happened to the Temple, which really means that on Tisha b'Av, we start becoming sad because of what happened to ourselves.

But it is even worse.

The truth is, on Tisha b'Av night we are crying — and G-d is crying as well. The Radomsker says that real people forget for a moment their own pain, and they *mamesh* pretend to be happy — for just a few minutes — in order to make it easier on their Father in Heaven. Because the destruction was hardest on Him.

If only we felt God's pain.

Whenever the Holy Vorker had to yell at his children, he would walk up to them first and say, "Sit down and make yourselves strong, because I have to yell at you." So, let's say, Mendele would sit down for a few minutes and get very strong, and then the Vorker would yell.

Imagine what kind of holy education this is. It seems to me that the Holy Vorker was telling his children, "I have to yell at you, because I am your father and I have to teach you. But I want to give you some time to prepare yourselves so you can take it."

G-d is our Father, and He wants to teach us. So sometimes He has to yell at us, to knock us off.

Do you know what the Ribbono Shel Olam did? Already when He created the world, He told Israel, "I have to yell at you on Tisha b'Av."

G-d gave us time to make ourselves strong so we could make it through.

A *Yiddele* once came to the *Heilege* Pshischer and asked for help. The Rebbe saw right away that the man needed to clean up his act, but he couldn't get through to him.

Now, the Pshischer was a top chess player. So he said to this *Yiddele*, "You know what? Let's play chess."

About two minutes into the game, the Pshischer made a mistake. So he said, "Please forgive me, I just wasn't paying attention. There is so much noise outside, and it bothered me. Really, just don't let it count against me this time."

But the *Yiddele* told him, "Okay, but this is a game. If you make a mistake, that's it."

Three minutes later, the Pshischer made a big mistake which put the other *Yiddele* in a tremendous position.

He said, "I can't concentrate; I'm having so much trouble right now. My wife is sick, my grandmother is sick, and also my mother-in-law."

"There are rules to this game," the Yid said. "You can't keep doing this."

The Pshischer did this five times.

Finally, the other Yid had had enough. He said, "Listen, I can't play with you."

The Pshischer looked at him closely and said,

"Tell me something. How many wrong moves in your life have you been making lately?"

Now let me ask you, how long did we have to suffer before we could receive the Torah? Two hundered and ten years. And how much suffering did we go through to get the Holy Land? Two thousand years — and we still haven't finished yet. Can you imagine how deep the Torah of Eretz Yisrael is, how strong the revelation of Mashiach is, that all that suffering was worth it? The holiness of the Pshischer story is to let you know: Please don't think that during the destruction, G-d isn't teaching me anything. The teaching of destruction is so strong that it has to get deeply into us.

You see what it is, for forty years in the desert we learned Torah, and then we came to the Holy Land. But our learning wasn't deep enough yet, because we went into exile for seventy years. We came back, but it still wasn't deep enough and we were exiled again. Right now we are *mamesh* in the final stages before Mashiach, and we are *mamesh* getting it. We are *mamesh* getting it. Tisha b'Av is the one day when, on the highest level, G-d is revealing to us the teaching of the destruction.

―∽―

What's the holiness of the Holy Wall?

It's so strange — it's just a broken wall, and yet you can see the Holy Temple. When you stand at the Kotel, you can *mamesh* see the Beis Hamikdash.

It isn't there, but we see it.

Behind all the brokenness, you see the Beis Hamikdash. Therefore, it is so holy.

Imagine we came to Yerushalayim and — lo and behold — there is this beautiful Holy Temple. It was just renovated by Max Cohen from Miami. He donated the paint, and even had an interior decorator. The Chief Rabbi has his office on the first floor. It's our pride and joy — such a beautiful building.

Honestly, how touching would it be? Would you shiver when you went there?

Do you understand why we shiver when we go to the Holy Wall?

We shiver because it's broken.

The Zohar Hakadosh says that even when the Holy Temple is rebuilt, it will still be broken.

How could God take away the holiness of the brokenness?

Do you know what happened to the broken tablets when Moshe replaced them with new ones? They were both there in the Holy Ark, the broken tablets and the "whole" full tablets — "*Luchos v'shivrei luchos munachim ba'aron.*" — "Both the tablets and the broken tablets were placed in the Ark."[25] It always has to be both — broken and not broken together.

G-d reveals Himself to broken people with a broken building.

&

I heard in Bobov that, during the War, the Bobover Rebbe was in the Jewish underground. And as part of his underground job, he worked for a Polish officer who was a secretary to one of the top Nazi generals. He was flying around in helicopters overlooking the concentration camps — you can't imagine how he felt! Then the craziest thing happened. One day, he discovered one torn page of *masechta Sanhedrin* in the Nazi general's garbage pail. Do you know what that means? One page!

He *mamesh* fell to the ground and covered the page. I'm sure that on Simchas Torah the Rebbe had a very high holiday. But he said, "How does even Simchas Torah compare to the joy I felt when I found one page of the Gemara in a Nazi general's office?!"

Tisha b'Av is the time of torn pages. So I'm *mamesh* begging you — please treasure those holy pages.

A similar story happened in Siberia. On Simchas Torah there, the Yidden were so desperate. They wanted to rejoice but they had no Torah.

In Siberia, what do you have? You have nothing.

Now listen to this — it happened right after the war:

The Yidden in Europe had so many *sefarim*, so many holy books. But the Nazis and the Russians tore everything apart. After the war, one Russian officer in Siberia got a letter from his son, and the letter was in an envelope. Would you believe that this envelope was made from a page torn out of siddur, a prayer book? *Gevalt!* The Russian

---

25 Tractate *Berachos* 8b

officer didn't know what the envelope was made from, so he threw it away. And a *Yiddele* discovered it lying on the ground — a thrown-away envelope with just a few lines from a siddur. He couldn't believe his eyes. He brought the envelope to all the Yidden, and do you know what they did on Simchas Torah night? Everybody had the great privilege of standing in the middle of a circle holding this envelope, with all the other *Yiddelach* dancing around him.

I don't know what it will feel like when Mashiach comes, but I'm sure those Yidden had a taste of Mashiach joy, even in the dark night of Siberia.

On Tisha b'Av, strange as it may seem, we have a chance to connect ourselves to the utmost pain of the *churban* Beis Hamikdash, and also to connect ourselves to the utmost joy of Mashiach's being born.

❧

As much as Tisha b'Av is about destruction, there is the strongest message of redemption within the pain. This is hinted to in the letter *tes* — the first letter of *Tisha* — itself. The shape of the letter *tes* is mostly closed, with just a little opening on the top. This teaches us that even if we think we are absolutely closed up, there is always a little opening on top, pointing toward Heaven…

❧

Tisha b'Av is the *yahrtzeit* of Reb Shlomo Molcho.

Reb Shlomo Molcho lived in the early 1500's and came from a family of Marrano's. He was raised Catholic and trained to be a bishop. When he was 21 years old, his father called him in and revealed to his son that they were really Yidden.

Reb Shlomo Molcho was still officially a monk, but secretly he began to learn Torah. Within a few years, he became a great Kabbalist. And, secretly, he became engaged to a girl who was also a Marrano, a secret Jew.

When this Reb Shlomo was twenty-six years old, he decided to go to Rome to tell the Pope to stop the Inquisition. But before he left for Rome, he gave his bride a letter which is *mamesh* incredible. He wrote to her, "Please bless me to come back. And please bless me to have the privilege of saving the lives and the *neshamahs* of our brothers and sisters. But..." he said, "if I don't come back, then I want you to know that I will return every Friday night to make *kiddush* for you."

Kodesh Kodashim, holy of holies.

Reb Shlomo Molcho arrived in Rome. It took a while to get an audience with the Pope. He waited and waited, until finally they told him his audience was set for Tisha b'Av.

Reb Shlomo thought that was a good sign, because Tisha b'Av is the day on which Mashiach is born.

So, on Tisha b'Av, he arrived for his audience. He walked in and said to the Pope, "I'm a Spanish monk. But really I'm a Marrano, and I've returned to being Jewish."

The Pope didn't want to hear another word: "You're a monk and you turned to Yiddishkeit?!" The Pope rang a bell, and they grabbed him. They took him to the market place, and threw him into the fire, right there on the spot.

It's just such a privilege to know that this *heilige neshamah* was one of us.

※

It is amazing — shocking really — to think about everything that happened on the saddest of days, Tisha b'Av. Before we entered the Holy Land, we sent twelve spies, one from every tribe. Ten spies came back and they said "It is a terrible country: It's beautiful, but we can't take it." Only two spies, Yehoshua from the tribe of Yosef and Caleb from the tribe of Yehudah, said "Ah, if G-d wants to give it to us, it's our land."

The night they came back was Tisha b'Av and the people started crying.

Feeling the Pain of Destruction ~ 51

That was the beginning, but the sadness didn't end there. Twice the Holy Temple was destroyed on this day, the Inquisition was decreed on Tisha b'Av; the first World War began on Tisha b'Av; in the Second World War, the first time Germany declared war and sent a message to Poland to surrender was on Tisha b'Av. It's unbelievable. It's still in the air.

But for us, Tisha b'Av will always be about the Holy Temple.

At the time of it's destruction, the blood ran from Jerusalem all the way down to the Jordan river. We don't know exactly how many people were living in Jerusalem at that time, but they killed many, many thousands.... some say millions... we have no idea.

It all traces back to the spies. Everything started then. So why did it start? It's all because ten people said something bad.

If you walk down the street, you'll notice many, many people — let's say half the world — that their light is destroyed. Sadly, most people are only the shadows of their own soul. A shadow of what they were, and what they could have been.

If you start investigating, going back to the roots of their lives, of their history, most probably you will find out that at one time or another, one person said something bad. That's how it started.

∼⋚∽

The Gemara says that Tisha b'Av is *"K'mi shemeiso mutal l'fanav"* you are *mamesh* standing by the coffin with the dead person in it.[26]

How do you talk to someone when you are mourning? You don't tell each other jokes. Even if you are so coarse that you can walk away and tell each other jokes, you don't do it right in front of the deceased. *Meiso mutal l'fanav*, when a dead person is lying in front of you — it is different. You can't speak that way.

Whether you are in Yerushalayim or Australia — the pain of Tisha b'Av is like *Mi shemeiso mutal l'fanav*, as if the Holy Temple is *mamesh*

---

26 Tractate *Ta'anis* 30b

lying in front of you. So when a dead person is lying in front of you be very careful. So on Tisha b'Av we need to be very careful with our words. That is why we ended up here in the first place.

❧

A teacher only has the right to teach us what is right and what is wrong. A father has different rights.

Obviously, on Tisha b'Av, the Ribbono Shel Olam is teaching us why the destruction of the Temple happened, why there is so much pain. Only He can teach us this — because He is our Father, and only a father has the right to teach us such things.

Still, G-d's teaching us about destruction and pain — it's all so hidden. A lot of times, we don't get it.

When Mashiach comes and everything becomes clear, we won't be able to understand why we didn't get G-d's messages while we were in exile.

We need Tisha b'Av to know something very holy. On Tisha b'Av, we don't learn Torah. Learning Torah is all about what is right and what is wrong. That is not what Tisha b'Av is about.

The teaching of Tisha b'Av is not regular learning. The teaching of Tisha b'Av is G-d's showing us all our brokenness, our destruction, everything which has gone wrong with us and with the world — and revealing, in His hidden way, what it all is for…

❧

The *Heilige* Rav Lazer Dovid was the grandson of the Holy Reb Dovid Lelover. This Rav Lazer Dovid was a *gevalt* rebbe. He would go to the Holy Wall every day of the year except one. The only day he would not go was on Tisha b'Av.

So finally his Chassidim asked him, "Rebbe, on Tisha b'Av all of Israel goes to the Holy Wall — and you don't go?"

Rav Lazer Dovid answered, "I'll tell you. Every morning when I go to the Kotel to *daven*, I say 'Good morning' to the Holy Wall. And I can hear the Holy Wall saying 'Good morning' back to me. On Shabbos, I say 'Good Shabbos' to the Wall, and I can hear the Kotel wishing me 'Good Shabbos.'

"But if I told the Holy Wall on Tisha b'Av what I would really want to say — and then I heard the Kotel answering me back — I wouldn't be able to live anymore. So today I just can't go."

*

You have to be very poor to not wear shoes, really poor. Even the poorest *schlepper* manages to get his own pair of shoes.

By not wearing my regular shoes on Tisha b'Av, I realize that unless I have the highest — I have nothing.

All year long we pretend we have something. We pretend to have a little Shabbos, a little *Yontiv*, a little holiday. I pretend to have a half a page of Gemara. I have a yarmulke, a skullcap, my wife lights Shabbos candles, and I think that's all there is to it. On Tisha b'Av, I realize that unless Mashiach comes, I'm just a poor *schlepper*.

On Tisha b'Av, I realize that my whole Yiddishkeit is nothing. Without the Beis Hamikdash, everything is empty. I *mamesh* need the Holy Temple.

So where do we go from here?

The Gemara says that the Ribbono Shel Olam can only put light into empty vessels. Let's say I have a piece of herring on my plate, and I put another little piece of herring on it. So my plate is full. The Ribbono Shel Olam will not give me a piece of herring unless I take my own piece off the plate.

Imagine that I come to the Ribbono Shel Olam and say, "Listen, I have a lot of Yiddishkeit in me. I'm sure You noticed, and I hope You are proud of me. I believe You noticed the way I *shuckle*, and the way I roll my eyes when I say *Shema Yisrael* is quite tremendous, no?" On Tisha b'Av, I take all of my old herring off my plate.

On Yom Kippur, I only confess my wrongdoings. When it comes

to my good doings, I seem to be okay. I think I did a lot of good things:

"Ribbono Shel Olam, let's not kid each other. I did a lot of good — I just made a few mistakes."

On Tisha b'Av, I am standing before G-d and saying, "Not only did I do wrong, I also didn't do anything good. *Mamesh* I obviously didn't accomplish anything, because the Beis Hamikdash is still not here."

Sometimes I talk to parents, and they tell me that, G-d forbid, some of their children have left Yiddishkeit. Of course they say, "I just can't understand it. My son had a tremendous Jewish education. He went to Sunday school, and at home, on Friday night, we always have chicken soup."

At one time a girl knocked on my door, and it was *mamesh* heartbreaking. Here was a Jewish girl with a shaved head — she had just been sworn in to become a Zen Buddhist monk. I'm telling you, it was just so heartbreaking to see. She was *mamesh* a *heilige neshamah*, a really holy soul, and she was really looking for something holy and deep. She told me about all she had gone through in her life with her parents. A few days later her mother called me and said, "I just can't understand my daughter. We gave her such a tremendous Jewish education." Do you know what it is? If only this woman would have come to me on a Tisha b'Av level… *Gevalt*.

On Tisha b'Av, I take off my shoes. There is something about shoes. Imagine you walk into a fancy restaurant. You can wear a tie and a tuxedo and smell of perfume, but if you are also barefoot the manager of the restaurant will say, "Listen, brother, you have no shoes on. You're nobody, you can't come in."

Try walking into a bank without shoes. You can't. They won't let you in. There is something to it, take it or leave it. If you have no shoes on, you're nobody. On Tisha b'Av, I'm a nobody.

Have you ever walked into a rich neighborhood and seen people sitting on their balconies? If you wave at them, do they wave back?

They think to themselves, *What chutzpah, what nerve! Who is he and what's he doing in my neighborhood?*

But when you walk in Harlem, you can sometimes see a couple of poor beggars there, some soul brothers sitting under a light. And when they see you they say, "Hey brother, hey brother."

These are poor people and they identify with poor people, one *schlepper* with another. Rich people don't talk to each other unless they are introduced. When a poor *schlepper* meets another *schnorer* by the door of shul, he doesn't say, "Listen, have we been introduced?"

Where does *sinas chinam*, baseless hatred, come from? Why do we hate each other? Because we have not been introduced. Do you need an introduction? People who walk barefoot don't need an introduction.

When do we need shoes? Only when we are walking. When you stand in one place you don't need shoes. All year long, I think I'm walking in G-d's way. I'm walking, so I need shoes.

On Tisha b'Av, I realize that I haven't been walking in G-d's way at all. I've been standing there like a dope. I think I have grown up so much. But on Tisha b'Av, I realize I'm standing still.

If I'm standing still, I don't need shoes.

Once, I had the privilege of being in Nice, France, on the Mediterranean coast, for Tisha b'Av. In Nice, especially in that part of France and Italy on the Riviera, there are a lot of *Sefardishe* Yidden who *mamesh* came from Spain.

One of the synagogues in Nice was an old shul where everybody *davened nusach Sefard*, according to the *Sefardi* tradition. This is not what we call today "*nusach Sefard*," which is how many Chassidim pray, but *nusach Sefardi* which is *mamesh* from Spain.

For the reading of Eichah, every *Yiddele* had a little candle. They *mamesh* sat on the floor and chanted Eichah. At the end of Eichah, before they said "*Lama lanetzach tishkacheienu*" — "Why will You forget us forever"[27] everybody blew out their lights; and they *mamesh* lay on

---

27   Eichah 5:20

the floor for a few minutes. It was so deep — *mamesh* all the lights went out. And then after a few minutes, everybody rekindled his or her little candle.

I looked around, and I noticed one simple *Yiddele*. He was still lying there, and he didn't kindle his light. He just lay on the floor in the dark for a long time.

He was feeling Tisha b'Av so deeply that he simply couldn't rekindle his light...

❧

Nobody has the chutzpah to say, "I really know what Shabbos is all about." All we have is a little taste.

If someone were to tell you "I really understand G-d perfectly, why He destroyed the Holy Temple; I really understand why He put 6 million in gas chambers..." — you know it can't be.

Maybe you can understand the Torah. If someone will tell you, "But listen, the prophets warned you — everybody says the Jews are not good, the destruction of the Temple is because we were so bad" — forget it. This isn't where it's at. This is not where it's at.

If someone says, "The 6 million, I know it was very bad, but most of them were assimilated, I really understand G-d perfectly, in fact, I would have done the same thing...."

How could someone talk like this? G-d forbid.

❧

The Gemara says, that after the destruction of the Temple, the Sages wanted to initiate that we shouldn't eat anymore, we don't get married anymore, *mamesh* we don't live, because this is what the destruction is all about.

The only thing is because it says "*Ein gozrim gezeirah she'ein hatzi-*

bur yachol la'amod bo,"²⁸ we don't decree a decree which the congregation cannot accept upon themselves.

You see what it is, most people don't know what the destruction is all about. For most people, it's just a sad thing, but they keep on doing their thing. So we can't do it. One day a year, on Tisha b'Av, it is *mamesh* that level that the lowest *Yiddele* says, "I *mamesh* refuse to eat," "I refuse to get married," "I refuse to wear shoes."

The Shabbos before Tisha b'Av is called Shabbos Chazon. The Hebrew word *chazon* which literally means a vision, is always about seeing the future, and Tisha b'Av is all about mourning the past.

How does Shabbos Chazon fit in with Tisha b'Av? What does the future have to do with the past?

Everybody knows that the Beis Hamikdash was destroyed because people didn't love each other. What does it mean not to love one another? It means I don't see you. If I hate you I don't see you, simple as it is!

The Beis Hamikdash was destroyed on a Saturday night. On the very last Shabbos, when the Yidden came to the Temple, they knew that the Beis Hamikdash would only be standing for a few more minutes. Can you imagine with how much love the people met each other in the Beis Hamikdash that last Shabbos? People who hated each other their whole lives, people who had spit at each other — can you imagine the way they saw each other on that last Shabbos? With so much love and longing to be close again. But you see, the love they felt that last Shabbos wasn't enough to keep the Beis Hamikdash standing, but *gevalt* has it been keeping us together for 2,000 years of exile.

So until today, every Shabbos Chazon the holiest thing happens to us Yidden. The Ribbono Shel Olam shows us every Jew who ever lived from Avraham Avinu until Mashiach. He shows us every *Yiddele*

---

28 Tractate *Bava Basra* 60b

and everything about each one's life in such a way that we go into Tisha b'Av filled with so much love for Am Yisrael.

Sometimes, we think that G-d created man to always be in Paradise. If we were always in Paradise, we wouldn't have needed the Torah of Mount Sinai because we would have known exactly what we had to do. Unfortunately, everything went wrong and we were kicked out of Gan Eden. So, we assume that the whole idea of the Messiah is only because mankind fell and we have to fix the world.

Nice little story, but it's not true.

There is a way-out Medrash that says like this: Adam was created on the sixth day, but *"V'Ruach Elokim merachefes,"* — the spirit of Mashiach was already around on the first day.[29] Adam wasn't there yet. Do you know what this means?

Right from the *first day*, Mashiach was already there. This is the way it was always supposed to be — this is the way it *is* supposed to be. There is no other way of learning except through chaos and destruction, and then bringing Mashiach. G-d could not say, "Let there be light," until we went through *sohu vavohu*, destruction and chaos.

When I was three years old, on Tisha b'Av, I saw my parents didn't eat. When you're two, you don't notice everything. When you're three, you start to notice.

So I saw that my parents weren't eating and I asked, "Why don't you eat?"

My father put me on his knee and started to explain to me everything. He talked about the Beis Hamikdash, and he made a big picture of the Holy Wall on the wall, and he explained to me everything.

---

29   *Bereishis Rabba* 2:4

I was so sad all day long. At night, I woke up at ten o'clock and saw my parents eating.

I started dancing like mad. My father asked me, "Why are you dancing?"

I said, "Because the Holy Temple is rebuilt!"

I thought that if my parents were eating again, it must be that the Temple was rebuilt!

My father smiled and explained some more.

So I asked, "Well, how can you eat if the Holy Temple is destroyed?"

My father got very sad. He was *mamesh* crying. He didn't say anything.

I asked him another question: "Are you doing something to rebuild the Holy Temple?" He then continued crying so, so much.

After a while, he said to me, "I want you to know that the same thing happened to me when I was three." The same thing — almost word for word.

And my grandfather said to my father, "You know something, the same thing happened to me when I was little."

How often do you feel that G-d is looking right at you?

How often do you feel that you are looking right at G-d?

How often do you feel that you are looking at each other?

If so, where does this looking take place?

Let's say I *mamesh* love someone the most. Can I sit in the middle of the street and look at them? No — because there is traffic. If I want to look at them without stopping, we have to have a bit of privacy — to go to our house.

The Beis Hamikdash was G-d's house, the place where we and the Ribbono Shel Olam looked at each other all the time. What happened when we were driven out of G-d's house and had to live on the street? We couldn't look at each other anymore.

Now imagine that I loved my wife the most, but suddenly we had a fight and we don't look at each other anymore. How am I going to fix it? Open your hearts in the deepest way. I say to her, "I wish we were still close, I wish we were still looking at each other. So let's sit in our house — here is the key — I just want us to look at each other again."

Do you know what happened at the last second before the Beis Hamikdash was destroyed? The Holy Temple was already burning, but all the young priests got together on the balcony. The High Priest was with them and he had the key to the Temple. Right before the balcony just fell into the fire, the High Priest said "G-d, we have guarded Your Holy Temple until the very last second. From now on You have to guard Your house."

He took the key and threw it up to heaven. And they saw a hand come down from heaven and take the key…

Listen to this very strange Medrash.

A king somehow got jealous of his wife. He thought that she wasn't being faithful to him. So he threw her out of the palace. She was standing outside, sitting by the door and wouldn't leave. Whenever he would leave the palace, she would see him, and whenever he would come back she would see him again.

He would say to her, "What a chutzpah, I threw you out and here you are sitting here. Whenever I walk out you look at me, whenever I come back you look at me."

She says to him "King, I'm just checking on you because I don't think any other woman wants you, because you always come back here." So he says to her "You know something, I love you so much, because of you all the other women don't look beautiful to me anymore." So she says to him "So why are you walking out all the time, aren't you looking for another woman?"

The Ribbono Shel Olam says to Yidden "*Gevalt*, because of you — the whole world doesn't look good to Me," and Yidden say back "Because of You, G-d, the whole world doesn't taste good anymore."

Yidden say "Ribbono Shel Olam, didn't You offer the Torah to the whole world, but nobody wanted it, just us?"

This is what it says *"Ani Hagever ra'ah oni."* What does *Ani Hagever* mean? Aren't we the only one that wants You? We are the only one who wants You. The Ribbono Shel Olam says back to us, "I can't go anywhere else because nothing looks beautiful to Me anymore."

On Tisha b'Av, people make a lot of noise crying *"Eichah!"* — the first word of the Book of Lamentations.

But let me ask you, friends, how does it sound to you?

It doesn't sound real. Why?

Because if you can hear it, it means that you don't *really* feel it. If you really feel the destruction of the Temple, the only way to mourn is by crying so loudly that *mamesh* nobody can hear it.

The Holy Shinover was the son of the *Heilege* Sanzer Rebbe.

Both Rebbes were out of this world, but the son, the Shinover, was very strict. He would say, "You can hang yourself on a nail, but if the *Shulchan Aruch* says that something has to be a certain way — then that's the way it has to be. Everything has to be according to the letter of the law." This is a very holy way.

So the Holy Sanzer himself was a little bit in awe of — maybe even a little bit afraid of — his son.

Everybody knows that the nine days before Tisha b'Av are very sad — we don't eat meat, we don't drink wine, and we don't make music.

But the Chassidim found a way to break the sadness a little bit. They would make a *siyum* — they would finish a tractate of the Talmud, which gave them an excuse to have a little *seudah*, a little feast. They even ate some meat and sang a little bit.

Still, nobody ever dared to have a *siyum* or to eat meat during the last three days before Tisha b'Av except for one Rebbe — Reb Shimon Yaroslaver.

Reb Shimon Yaroslaver was one of the top pupils of the Seer of Lublin.

Do you know when he would make a feast for a *siyum*? At the *seudas mafsekes*, at the last meal before Tisha b'Av, when you're supposed to sit on the floor and eat a hardboiled egg with dust and ashes on it. That's when Reb Shimon would finish a tractate of the Gemara and make a feast. He even ate meat — and then he would start singing, "Ribbono Shel Olam, please rebuild the Holy Temple." His singing would sometimes last until very late into the night of Tisha b'Av. Of course, he would stop eating when the official time of the fast began, but he would only begin chanting Eichah way into the night.

All his life, the Holy Sanzer wanted so much to be at that *seudah* in Yaroslav, but he was afraid to go because of his son, the Shinover, who was so straight.

Finally, he decided, "I don't care what my son will say. I have to go." At the time, the Shinover was still very young. The Holy Sanzer was only about fourteen years older than his son; he was then around thirty years old, and the Shinover was a teenager.

Anyway, that year early in the morning before Tisha b'Av, the Shinover saw that his father was preparing to go somewhere. So he asked his father, "Where are you going?"

The Sanzer answered, "Nowhere, really. I'll be right back."

But the Shinover wasn't stupid. He knew something was up.

So he said, "Tell me something. Are you by any chance going to that most horrible thing in the world, the *seudah* of Reb Shimon Yaroslaver?"

"Yes," admitted the Sanzer. "In fact, that is where I'm going."

The Shinover started thinking, Oy gevalt, what is happening to my father? He's going all the way down.

He didn't say anything, but the Sanzer could tell what he was thinking by the expression on his face. So he said to his son, "Listen, I'm going no matter what you think. You can go with me if you want, but only on one condition. You have to promise to keep your mouth shut. If you don't want to be there, then don't come. But if you come, then promise you'll be quiet. Don't make me any trouble."

The Shinover promised he would not open his mouth, and since he was so straight — when he promised something, then that's what happened.

So the Sanzer and the Shinover set out for the little village of Yaroslav. They arrived in the late afternoon, and found everybody preparing for the *siyum* and the feast. Everyone, including the two visitors, went into the *beis medrash*. The Sanzer was a little bit nervous because of his son, so he sat in a back row. But the Shinover went up to the front and sat down right next to the Yaroslaver.

Reb Shimon finished his tractate of the Talmud and the *seudah* began. The Shinover just sat there with a sour face. Naturally, he wouldn't eat any of the meat — in fact he didn't eat anything — such a thing was unheard of. But upset as he was, he could still bear it, and he didn't say what he was thinking.

It got later and later. The Shinover looked out of the window and saw that the day was over and Tisha b'Av had begun. Suddenly the Yaroslaver stood up and started singing like mad. Now the Shinover couldn't hold back any longer. He too stood up and he shouted,

"This is blasphemy, absolute blasphemy! It's bad enough that you eat meat during the Nine Days when you're not allowed to. But to sing on Tisha b'Av?! You're all crazy!" And he ran out of the room.

About two o'clock in the morning, the Shinover, who was standing right outside the door to the *beis medrash*, heard the Chassidim start *davening* the evening prayer. He had long before given up on Reb Shimon, and he had given up on his father — they were hopeless cases. But he had to say Eichah on Tisha b'Av, so he had waited for hours for a minyan, and went back in the room and *davened Maariv* together with everyone else.

After the evening prayer everybody sat on the floor, and Reb Shimon Yaroslaver began to say *Eichah*.

He said only that one word, and he *mamesh* keeled over. It hurt him so much that he fainted. He just couldn't bear the pain. Everybody jumped up like mad to try to help him.

This is how the Shinover described it later:

"Everybody tried to bring the Holy Yaroslaver back to life. They worked on him for about ten hours, but they couldn't get him back. I was standing over the tzaddik, and my tears were flowing like never before.

And I was praying, "*Gevalt*, was I wrong! Please, Ribbono Shel Olam, let this holy man live. Because nobody knows the pain of all of Israel more than the *Heilege* Reb Shimon Yaroslaver."

Sometimes, you have a good *kasha*, a very deep question, about the world — but then you start giving stupid answers. It's sweet, but that's not where it's at. I hate to say bad things, but there are some people who have a whole theory about the 6 million. For everything they have a great theory — a theory for why there was a Yom Kippur War, a theory for this, a theory for that.

If you think about it a little bit, it becomes clear:

What do I really know? I don't know anything, and Mashiach will not come until I realize I *mamesh* don't know anything and I don't know what to do.

When we realize this, we'll know more than we thought we knew when we thought we had answers to the hard questions.

Think about it: Where was there a higher revelation of G-d, on Mount Sinai or in the Holy Temple?

The holiness of Mount Sinai was that everything was clear. It was a very high revelation, but it was on the level of being clear.

When we came to the Beis Hamikdash and started *davening*, we realized it just has to be deeper than whatever we thought was clear to us; that can't be all there is to it. So I know the whole

Torah, I stood holy at Mount Sinai. But the world is still broken. I kept Shabbos, I put on tefillin (phylacteries), I learned Gemara — and I still don't know what it's all about. It is so much bigger than us. How can we understand it?

Sometimes you take a *Yiddele* and you tell him, "You have to keep Shabbos, put on tefillin, do a few tricks here and a few tricks there — and that's all there is to it. This is all there is to Yiddishkeit."

Do you really think that this is all the Ribbono Shel Olam has to tell you? There has to be more to it than that….

What's Yom Kippur all about? On Yom Kippur, I come to the Holy Temple and say to the Ribbono Shel Olam, "I tried my best to be a good *Yiddele*, and it didn't work. Please, G-d, You have to reveal to me something deeper than that."

What's Tisha b'Av all about? The destruction of the Temple tells me that I know I need something deeper, but the problem is that I don't know where to go.

Imagine, G-d forbid, that somebody is sick. He calls up the doctor and the doctor gives him some medicine. A week later he comes back and says to the doctor, "Listen, brother, please give me better medicine because the first medicine you gave me didn't work. I need something stronger."

Every Yom Kippur is stronger medicine. I come and say "I did this wrong, I sinned here and sinned there — please give me some strong medicine." When the Temple was standing, the Kohen Gadol, the High Priest, would go into the big drug store up in the Holy of Holies and get some strong medicine. On Tisha b'Av, I am sick to the core. I'm coming to the site of the Holy Temple and, I have no medicine. I don't know what to do.

The deepest revelation comes down on Tisha b'Av. We say to G-d, "We went through so much for You, Ribbono Shel Olam. We went through so much that there has to be something special about the whole thing. I don't know yet what it is… but there has to be something to it that is so deep."

Imagine how much we go through to be in the Holy Land. So, so much. In Israel, we're free. No one can tell us what to do. We can pluck Jewish oranges, but do you really think this is what it's all about? It's got to be deeper than that. The Holy Land is about plucking oranges?

Reb Nachman says it's a very high revelation to know that I don't know what to do.

What's the difference between a low doctor and a high doctor? You walk into a low doctor, and he has medicine for any sickness in the world. He thinks that he can cure everything. A high doctor is good, very good, but he knows he can't cure everything. Sometimes, he says, "I don't know… I just don't know."

Reb Nachman says that when you come to a little doctor with a headache, he examines you and tells you to take aspirin.[30] A high doctor says, "Listen, I can give you aspirin, but this is not the point. I'd like to know why you have a headache. Let's examine it."

Hashem wants all of us to be top doctors.

A *Yiddele* can say, "Listen, the Beis Hamikdash is destroyed. Let's have the chief rabbis get together and then maybe we can rebuild it."

Another *Yiddele*, a better doctor, says, "Listen brother, what you are saying is not enough. You have to examine *why* it was destroyed."

Someone might say, "Listen, there is no Yiddishkeit in Israel. Let's make a sign calling for *tzniyus*, for modesty, and another one for *shemiras Shabbos*, another one for this, another one for that — and that will take care of it."

But another *Yiddele* answers, "Brother, don't kid yourself. Let's find out why things are the way they are. Because we don't know. All the pain, all the children, all the sadness. We don't know why it all happens. We really don't know."

That is what it is all about. Not knowing. Knowing we don't know. That is the greatest revelation.

---

30   *Likutei Moharan* 2 7:6

If someone is *chas v'shalom* sick, there are two ways of curing them. If someone goes to a doctor saying "Fix me, cure me, my *kishkes* hurt me, my heart hurts me, everything hurts me," the doctor gives a few pills and fixes the person.

This is very good, but it's not so deep. Imagine if someone would come to the doctor and say "I don't just want you to cure me, is it possible to X-ray me and so that I should see how sick I really am?"

On Yom Kippur, we come to the Ribbono Shel Olam saying we did so much, everything we did wrong. We do *teshuvah* and everything is broken and destroyed. We come to the Ribbono Shel Olam saying "fix me again." So the Ribbono Shel Olam gives us a few pills. We blow the shofar, we fast, we do *teshuvah*. All kinds of good pills and He fixes us.

But once a year, the Ribbono Shel Olam is X-raying us and we *mamesh* see what we did, it's on Tisha b'Av. We see what we did! We destroyed the world, we destroyed the Beis Hamikdash, we destroyed the holiest thing in our hearts. We know what we did. But when we see it... *oy*, that is hard. That is painful.

How come one of our parents or grandparents had to be in Auschwitz but not me?

Am I so special that I didn't have to be there?

How come my great-great-grandfather was in the Inquisition? Am I so special that I can just live my life, wake up in the morning, drink a little bit of coffee, *daven*, do something else?

It doesn't sound right. It's got to be deeper than that.

Some of the kabbalists explain: In one of your reincarnations, you have to go through *mesirus nefesh*.

One time, maybe you were in Auschwitz, the Inquisition, maybe you were there during the destruction of the Holy Temple.

One time, in one of your reincarnations you were there, you went through it.

The story of the pain of the destruction of the Temple is not somebody else's story. Deep down, maybe my mind doesn't know, but my soul remembers my story. Everyone went through something.

Sometimes, you meet people and there are such deep things between you. Maybe you were in the same synagogue during the time of the Crusaders. You never know... you never know.

Let's hope that most of us went through it already last time. Right now, we are just fixing the last few little things... hopefully.

I hope you realize friends, it's not simple to be a *Yiddele*. *Gevalt*, it's so deep, *gevalt* is it deep to be a *Yiddele*.

To be a child of Yitzchak who was lying on the altar, you think you just read a few lectures about Judaism and you are already a son of Yitzchak?

Not so simple.

Whenever Moshe Rabbeinu talked to the Yidden it says, "*Daber el Bnei Yisrael*" — "Speak to the Children of Israel." It never says "to all of Israel". But the Shabbos before Tisha b'Av we read that Moshe Rabbeinu spoke "*L'kol Yisrael*" — "to all Israel."[31] Why the difference?

I want to share something very deep with you.

When Moshe spoke to the Children of Israel, every *Yiddele* heard exactly what Moshe Rabbeinu meant to tell him. Imagine that Chaim, Simcha, and Shprintza are sitting in a room, and Moshe Rabbeinu is talking. He talks to all of them, yet Chaim hears what he needs to hear, Simcha hears what he needs to hear, and Shprintza hears what she needs to hear. But none of them receive what is intended for the others.

On Mount Sinai, G-d spoke to us in such a way that every *Yiddele* knew what he had to do. It was no one's business what G-d told anyone else to do.

The teaching of Tisha b'Av is something else. The teaching of Tisha

---

31   Devarim 1:1

b'Av is so deep that unless I *mamesh* feel the pain of every *Yiddele* — what he has to go through in his life — I am disconnected from the Beis Hamikdash. Tisha b'Av is all about *"L'kol Yisrael"* — "to all of Israel."

So you see what it is, we'll need Tisha b'Av until we hear not only what is meant for each of us — but when we also hear what is meant for everyone else.

The Holy Pshischer would go to the city of Dantzig every year. It was officially for business, but, unofficially, he would find some outstanding holy souls and turn them on.

One night, he was going out with his friends to the theater, and they all had a program in their hands. The Holy Pshischer was looking at his program when one of his friends asked him, "Are you still going to your Rebbe, the Holy Yid Hakadosh?"

"Of course," the Pshischer answered. "How could I not?"

His friend said, "You yourself know everything too, you know all the holy books. Why do you need a Rebbe?"

So the Pshischer said, "Let me ask you. You have a program in your hand. Why do you have to go to the theater?"

You see, we have a split between our heads and the deepest depths of our souls.

We can read all the books, we can know everything in our heads — but it takes so long for our head-knowledge to get into our insides.

This is where we need a Rebbe to help.

And here I want you to open your hearts in the deepest depths.

If Eve had not eaten from the forbidden fruit of the Tree of Knowledge, then she could have had children without pain — because she would have known what it was all about. Knowing and feeling and sensing would all have been one.

When she ate from the Tree, she separated her knowledge from the deepest depths of her soul. So G-d said to her, "I'm sorry to tell you, but if you ever want to be close to your children, you will have to go through so much pain."

Why? Knowledge that is only in the head isn't enough for a mother to be close to her children. The head-knowledge has to get into the depths of her. And, sadly enough, this only happens through pain....

On Tisha b'Av, we correct the Tree of Knowledge. Do you know how we do this? We don't learn, because we are afraid we will learn the words but we still will do the same thing again, learning from the Tree of Knowledge again. We need to get out of this knowledge business — we have to get into life in the deepest depths.

As an example, imagine I have a library of 40,000 books and I've read every book. So I think I know all about life.

Then, one day, I'm on a ship and G-d forbid it starts to sink. Suddenly, I see in the water one little piece of wood. I grab it and hold on to it — and it saves my life. Now let me ask you — what taught me more about life — all those 40,000 books, or that piece of wood I held on to when I was drowning?

Do you understand?

The 40,000 books are the Tree of Knowledge.

The little piece of wood is "*Eitz chayim hee lamachazikim bah*" — the Torah is "a Tree of Life to those who are holding it."[32] This is the Tree of Life if I hold on to it. This is the Torah when it gets into the depths of my soul.

And this is the teaching of Tisha b'Av.

༄

At the end of the First World War, there were holy tzaddikim who saw with their holy eyes what is happening.

One of the biggest rebbes was the holy Dzikover. At the end of the First World War he said "I see a darkness coming into the world, I

---

32 Mishlei 3:18

don't want to be there. I don't want to be there," and he passed away the next day.

At the end of the First World War, there was a certain nation, the Germans, who we thought were civilized. They weren't. They came into Galicia, and they said that twelve Jews were spies for the other side, and they killed them.

The Jews came to the Holy Bluzhover Rebbe and were *mamesh* crying. The Bluzhover says "Can you please close the door." He had this big long pipe, and he was smoking away. The whole room was full of smoke.

Then he said, "Please remember what I'm telling you. You are talking to me about twelve Jews? Do you know that a time is coming and they will kill millions. I don't want to be there. Please G-d, I don't want to be there."

Now listen to this. The next day he took off, he didn't want to be in this world anymore. Such a holy tzaddik, and he said that they will kill millions. Why didn't they leave? Why didn't they do something?

It's the strangest thing in the world. The next day, they asked each other, "What did the Rebbe say yesterday?" and nobody could remember. They did not remember what the Rebbe said yesterday.

How do I know the story? There is a *Yiddele* who now lives in Boro Park. One of the people who were there in 1918, strangely enough, went through Auschwitz and survived. He came to Yerushalayim, went to the Holy Wall.

He was crying so much over his family, and everything else. Suddenly, while he was standing by the Holy Wall, suddenly, it came back to him: In 1918 the Bluzhover told us already what will be.

The prophets at the end of the First Temple all saw what's happening, and they said "Ribbono Shel Olam, I don't want to be there, I refuse to be there."

There was one prophet who said "Ribbono Shel Olam, I want to be there. If everybody is there, I have got to be with them, I've got to see it." This was Yirmiyahu.

So the first two chapters of Eichah were written before the destruction of the Temple, when he saw prophetically what's going to happen. The third, fourth, and the fifth were written after.

"*Ani hagever ra'ah oni,*"[33] I was there, I was there.

When they chained all the Jews and brought them to slave markets, Yirmiyahu was standing there, crying, and saying, "Why didn't you listen? Why didn't you listen to me?"

In the first chapter of Eichah, Yirmiyahu tells us prophetically about the destruction of the Temple. It was clear to him why the destruction took place.

Listen to this: Suddenly, we were so lonely.

There are two kinds of loneliness.

If you never had anybody in the world and don't like being alone — that's one kind of loneliness.

If you were so close to somebody and suddenly he or she is gone, that's even worse. This is the loneliness of the book of Eichah.

In the first part, Yirmiyahu is crying out. At one time there was a Beis Hamikdash. The whole world was there. And now, suddenly there's nobody.

In the second part, the second chapter, Yirmiyahu is crying over all the beauty that was taken away from us. I mean, even that which we have is not beautiful anymore. It's just the saddest thing — everything became ugly.

And then sections *gimel, daled,* and *heh,* the third, fourth, and fifth chapters, are just the most heartbreaking. Yirmiyahu says, "*Ani hagever ra'ah oni*" — I am the man who was there — I was *mamesh* there during the destruction, I saw it. To be there during the *churban* Beis Hamikdash... you can barely make it.

But can you imagine someone seeing the destruction of the Holy Temple with prophetic eyes... it was *mamesh* a miracle that Yirmiyahu stayed alive despite everything he saw — literally, a miracle.

---

33 Eichah 3:1

A lot of people walk around saying "Thank G-d we are now back in Israel, we can do what we want, what do we need the Holy Temple for? Isn't it great, we have the Wall!"

If you are just a little bit plugged in, seeing the Holy Wall is *mamesh* heartbreaking.

Imagine if I love someone very much and then, G-d forbid, we have a fight, and we don't see each other anymore. I'm heartbroken. But I'm in a different place so I can forget a little bit… I try to ignore the pain.

Now imagine if we were accustomed to meet in a certain place. I'm coming back to that place and the other person isn't there, that's *mamesh* heartbreaking. When you stand by the Holy Wall and the Ribbono Shel Olam isn't there the way we want Him to be… it hurts in such a deep way.

Now let's say again that I love someone very much, but we had a fight and stop seeing each other. Of course, deep down, we really still love each other. And we're both thinking that all we need to do is to meet again and everything will be okay. That's what we're hoping, at least. But it might take more than that. Imagine that we really do meet, but we're not so close anymore. It isn't the same.

That's when I *mamesh* realize — *gevalt*, what did I do? Do you know how much that hurts? That's much deeper than the whole thing. If I meet that person I was so close to, and suddenly I'm not so close anymore, then I realize the destruction I caused. When I'm not in Yerushalayim, I think that all I need is for the Ribbono Shel Olam to take me back to Yerushalayim and everything will be fixed, but then I'm back in Yerushalayim and I realize its more than that. *Gevalt*, what did I do?

So the thing is like this; I feel it in a very strong way.

Tisha b'Av is the time when the Ribbono Shel Olam in His goodness is *mamesh* showing us what we did wrong. The fixing will be done later, the fixing begins to take place at noon on Tisha b'Av. Till twelve o'clock, it's not a time for fixing, it's a time for X-raying. The Ribbono Shel Olam shows us what we did.

On Tisha b'Av night after *Maariv*, you sit down and you say "*Eichah yashvah badad*,"[34] how did this happen to us, what happened to us. One Tisha b'Av night, the *Heilige* Reb Avraham the *malach*, the son of the Mezritcher Maggid, sat down and said those three words, and he couldn't move. He sat there till Tisha b'Av at twelve o'clock, without moving. You can imagine how holy he was because exactly at *chatzos*, the split second when Mashiach can be born, he got up.

When you feel the pain in such a real way, you also sense the salvation.

When you feel the destruction, really feel it, you sense the redemption.

---

34 Eichah 1:1

3
Missing Something When it's Already There

I want to share something with you that I heard from an Alexander chassid. The chassid said, "Do you know how holy Shabbos was in the town of Alexander? The way the Rebbe sang *Shalom Aleichem*, the way he sang *Eishes Chayil* — it was absolutely out of this world. After the *davening*, we all came up to the Rebbe and said, '*l'chayim*', and we would hold his holy hand. The Rebbe would look at us, right into the depths of our *neshamahs*. Do you know how much he cleaned our souls when he looked at us, how much he put our souls in the right place?"

The chassid paused, and then he said, "Okay, this was all very holy. But let me tell you. When I was in Auschwitz, somehow, one way or the other, I suddenly found myself together with ten other Alexander Chassidim. Every Friday night, we would sit and tell each other how good Shabbos was in Alexander.

"Can you imagine how deep it was — the way we relived those Shabbosess?

"It was much deeper than the way we felt when we actually were in Alexander...."

So when did Shabbos in Alexander *mamesh* get into these Chassidim, into the deepest depths of their *neshamahs*?

When there was no Alexander anymore…

In one sense, we only truly connect to things when we lose them. We miss them when they are gone.

On a deeper level, we can miss things while we have them.

Those who live in Yerushalayim never have the privilege of missing Yerushalayim and those who are not often in Yerushalayim have the great privilege of missing Yerushalayim.

Still, it is not 100 percent true because how do you know how much you love somebody?

If you miss them while you are talking to them.

When you love somebody very much, it makes you whole and it also breaks your heart.

Gevalt, does Yerushalayim break my heart.

Gevalt, Shabbos makes me whole — and it also breaks my heart.

Why was the Holy Temple destroyed? Because we stopped being broken over it. We didn't miss it while it was standing. We weren't broken over it.

What's an assimilated Jew? Yiddishkeit is beautiful; I like it. It is a beautiful way of life. I'm proud of being a Jew. Do you know what that means? It means that it doesn't break your heart.

So, sadly enough, the Master of the World had to destroy the Holy Temple. He had to break the Holy Temple so that we should feel the brokenness.

When you miss something, you are broken. Even while you are in Yerushalayim and it's whole, it's broken.

The secret of life is that everything should be whole and broken.

Sweetest friends, from time to time, we should have the privilege of being broken, of being broken over the Torah, broken over Yerushalayim.

There are two kinds of longing in the world.

Imagine if I don't know anything about Yiddishkeit. I don't know anything about G-d. I am just coming out of Egypt. G-d says to me "I'm taking you to Mount Sinai," I'm longing for it so much. This is a very deep kind of longing.

There is an even deeper kind of longing. I am already on Mount Sinai and G-d is saying to me that there really is one G-d, "I am the Lord your G-d." At that moment I am longing to know G-d in such an incredible way.

Let's put it this way, on our level.

Imagine that I have not met my soul mate yet. I am longing so much that I should find my soul mate. Very deep level of longing.

Still, there is a deeper kind of longing — and this happens once I meet my soul mate. It's even deeper.

Imagine that I have not met my soul mate yet and someone asks me "What are you longing for?" I can talk to them about it, I could tell them how lonesome I am, looking for my soul mate, etc. Once I meet my soul mate and I miss her very much, if I really love her — I am not going to discuss it with anybody. It is beyond words.

Anything which is really deep in your heart, you can't talk about, it's a profanation. On Pesach, G-d took us out from Egypt. We didn't know anything, we were just in a period of holy wanting. We could talk about it, we wanted Him so much.

On Shavuos, something awesome takes place. We are longing for the Torah when we already have it — this is the deepest depths. Imagine if G-d blesses me that I can learn a bit of Gemara and I *mamesh* want to learn, if I can read Chumash in Hebrew, I am sitting over this passage and I really want to learn it.

When I find my soul mate and I want to be much closer to her — that is the deepest depths there is. Missing what you have. It's so deep.

When you really understand something, then it's clear to you that you don't understand it at all.

Every person is made up of two sides. One side is what I have, and the other side is what I don't have. The side which I don't have is not simply not having something. I am longing for it so much.

There is one part of me which is completely unfulfilled. There is a part of me which I have, which is there, but there is a little part of me which is *mamesh* longing.

If I long for a hundred dollars, that means I don't have it.

But think about it. How could I long for something holy? If I would not be connected to it, I would not long for it. I only long for it because I already have it.

I don't long for a person to whom I have no connections, I only long for a person who I am so connected to.

In this way, I want what is already mine.

Say it another way: How do you know if something is really yours?

If you miss it while you have it — if while you have it, you are longing for it — that means that it is really yours.

Why is Yerushalayim so holy? Because while you are standing by the Holy Wall, you miss the Holy Wall so much. While you are in Jerusalem, you cry for it while you are there.

Sometimes, we don't know how much we want something that we already have. When do we realize how much we want it? When it is taken away from us, G-d forbid.

Tisha b'Av is the day that everything was taken away from us — because, if you think about it, everything is connected to *churban* Beis Hamikdash. When we think about the Temple we lost, we realize how much we want it. We know how much it means to us.

Don't ever lose hope, G-d only took it away from us in order that we should know how much we want it.

Imagine that you're learning Gemara, and you are really into the *sugya* (topic). You are walking on the street and someone takes away the tractate you are learning. It tears out your soul — the *sefer* means so much to you.

It happened to me a lot of times in life, I'm learning from a *sefer*, and then suddenly I lost the *sefer*. I look for it like mad. Thank G-d, I find it again — but I treat it a little differently now.

So what is it that I receive after I go through Tisha b'Av? The holiness is that we never forget how much it means to us. The secret is that the one moment when we lost, it is still with us.

※

What happened to us during the long exile?
Why did we die so often for G-d?
During the time of the Beis Hamikdash, G-d could also have done something similar: People would come and they'd say "Listen, if you don't convert, if you don't become a pagan, I'll kill you…" In the time of the Beis Hamikdash, it didn't happen much, why is it like this in exile?

The explanation is that the whole idea of exile is that I myself don't know how much it all means to me. The whole 2,000-year exile is all about dying for G-d — just so that I should know myself how much it means to me.

Everybody knows that the whole *Churban Beis Hamikdash* came about with the spies.

What was wrong with the spies? They wanted to go to Israel, but they saw how hard it would be… If I love someone so much, but there are so many problems… What does that mean? It means that I don't want to marry them, not fully. I want to, but I want it without problems.

The spies come back with a lot of problems, "The neighbors are strong…"[35] The spies were not lying — the Torah never says that they were lying. They were right! There were giants. It didn't mean just physically the people were giants — the spies knew how hard it is to come to Eretz Yisrael.

They weren't lying. They were prophets, they foresaw prophetically that for us to be in Eretz Yisrael is so hard. It's unbearably hard.

Yehoshua comes and says "*Im chafetz banu Hashem,*" "If G-d wants

---

35 Bamidbar 13:28

us to be there, we'll be there."[36] So the whole thing began with thinking *If there's a problem, forget it*. But you know what this means, if I face difficulty and assume I should give up — it means it's not that important to me.

How does something become important to you? Do you long for it once you already have it?

Imagine that one time I kept Shabbos, and I stopped. What was missing? My problem was not the first Shabbos which I didn't keep. My problem was because, even while I kept Shabbos, it wasn't 100 percent.

When people get divorced, the problem doesn't start the moment they get divorced. Their problem began at the wedding itself. When they were with their new spouse under the *chuppah*, they didn't miss them yet. They weren't longing for what they already had.

I know a broken *Yiddele*. He had one child before Auschwitz, and this child was two years old. All he has left is a pair of his baby's shoes.

Gevalt, gevalt, gevalt.

The holiest broken tablets, maybe, in the world.

Can you imagine when Mashiach comes, and all the people will be revived, he'll meet this baby again? While the baby was alive, the shoes weren't so deep to him. Why would they be? Just a pair of shoes. But now....

What's so special about being in exile?

Things seem meaningless, suddenly they're the most important things in the world.

How is it that I'm able to wait for 2,000 years for Yerushalayim to be rebuilt?

Because my connection to Yerushalayim comes from such a high place. I can wait forever.

---

36   Bamidbar 14:8

I'm not going to sit and wait for a bagel for two hours. It's not worth it. Why? Because life is more important.

How long will you sit and wait for a friend? You'll sit as long as they are important to you. Some friends are "two-hours" important to you, others are "three-hours." Another is even important "five-hours." But I'm not going to sit for three days.

Can you imagine waiting for somebody for 2,000 years?

It must be very important.

Life itself is very important. Life itself.

We always think of life in terms of, "what can I do with it?" Because, for us, life is money, and money has no real value — only what you can do with it. For one dollar, I can buy Coca Cola and an ice cream. For five dollars, I can even have blintzes.

Life itself is not what you're doing with it. Life is life itself. Eretz Yisrael is the land of life. Yerushalayim is the city of life. For life itself, you wait forever.

You miss it. You pray for it. You long for it, but you wait for it. If you're connected to life, there is no reason to get angry. Why should I get angry? Nothing is that important to take away my life, because when I'm angry I'm dead.

I'm interested in living. I'm interested in Yerushalayim.

I have it, but I want it.

I'm alive, but I long to live.

4 G-d Never Left

There was once a couple in Rome who loved each other very much, but they were always fighting. So, after a while, they decided to separate and see what would happen. The wife said she was going back to her mother in Florence, and he would go traveling around Europe.

They locked up the house, but he promised that every Friday he would send her a letter.

She gets his first letter and is very surprised. He wrote, "After we closed the house in Rome, I went to Paris. I met this very nice lady. To make a long story short, we're going to get married. I will write you back again next week."

Next week, he writes her a letter, "I told you about that young lady I met in Paris, but that was not the real thing. This week I am in Hamburg and this is the real thing. I met this young lady and we're going to get married." Every week it was a different city and a different girl.

The wife was so broken. She thought he loved her. She wasn't with him for two weeks and already he is going to marry someone else.

She decided that for a few weeks, she will not stay with her mother and read all those letters. She'd had enough. Things weren't so good with her parents anyway — they were making her crazy with their questions: When are you getting a divorce? What is making you wait?

So she decided to go back to Rome to the house where she had lived with her husband. When she got there, at first she just walked around from room to room, and every corner in the house was so precious. She remembered sadly her time there, thinking; *Oh, when I lived here I was so happy. Everything was so beautiful.*

She's thinking, *At least here I will be safe from his letters, it just breaks my heart.*

She comes into his study and sees a light burning. She sees him sitting by his desk writing her more crazy letters. *Gevalt* is he happy to see her!

The wife asked him, "What are you doing here?"

He says to her "You know something, I never left… I never left. I was just making up those letters so that you shouldn't think that I am sitting here waiting for you. I made up those crazy letters so you wouldn't know I was still here. And I got people to send them to you from all those cities. I've been sitting here waiting for you the whole time…"

Do you realize how deep this is?

You sit in exile in New York, Sydney, or Rome, or anywhere across the world, and you get all those crazy letter from G-d that seem to say, "I am not taking care of the Yidden." So many letters: the destruction of the Temple, the Inquisition, the 6 million.

It really seems like G-d is telling us that He isn't taking care of His People anymore. So you cry out, "*Oy vey*, Ribbono Shel Olam — How could You do all this to us?"

Do you really think that G-d forgot us?

When you come back to the Holy Wall in Yerushalayim, you see that G-d is still there. The *Zohar HaKadosh* says "*Me'olam lo zazah HaShechinah*,"[37] G-d's Divine Presence never left the Holy Wall. Even when we are here in exile, G-d is sitting there and waiting for us. It's just a misunderstanding.

G-d never ever really left the Beis Hamikdash. He is still right

---

37 *Zohar Shemos* 5b

here. Even while we have been so long in exile, G-d has kept sitting there in the Holy City, by the Holy Wall, waiting for us....

⁕

In a time of war, you have to send a secret message to the king, and he has to send a secret message to his soldiers.

He doesn't send a general dressed with all his medals. He sends a *schlepper*. No one expects the *schlepper* to send a message, so he can get through. No one stops him.

We are in the last war between good and evil in the world. We are little messengers from one Jew to another, from G-d to the Jews, and back.

Do you know who G-d chooses to give over messages? Little *schleppers*, like you and me. We don't look like much and people don't think we are anything, but we look low enough that no one stops us.

We get through!

We are the messengers, but what message should we carry?

The greatest message is to go to every Jew in the world and to let them know that the Holy Temple is not destroyed.

It just looks destroyed. The Holy Temple is right there waiting for you.

The greatest message from one Jew to the other is that the Torah lives. The Torah is alive. Every word of the Torah is so alive.

⁕

We are lonesome for G-d, but is G-d lonesome for us?

The Gemara says something very deep. The Gemara says, "*Oy lahem l'banim shegalu me'al shulchan avihem*" — the lonesomeness of the destruction is like children who were taken away from their parents' table, G-d forbid.[38]

---

38 Tractate *Berachos* 3a

When children leave their parents' home, they make their own homes. They miss their parents, but they can make their own homes and fill them with light.

Imagine if, when children leave their parents' home, their parents would say, "Okay, our children are gone and this house feels empty. So let's build another house." They can't do it. They just can't do it.

We *Yiddelach* went into exile, but one way or another we built synagogues, we built little houses for ourselves.

What did G-d do when His House was destroyed? Did He build another house? No... because it's very simple. How can a father just build another house because his children have left? Any other house would be just as empty without them....

How do we know most deeply that G-d is our Father? Because He never built another house.

The difference between the Ribbono Shel Olam and us Yidden is very simple. When we were driven out into exile, we didn't have to live on the street. We had somewhere to live, even if we were living in somebody else's house.

The Ribbono Shel Olam doesn't even have that. Since the Holy Temple was destroyed, the Ribbono Shel Olam has no home....

Reb Nachman was working throughout his whole life to reach the level of doing everything as if it was for the first time.

There is a letter from the *Heilige* Reb Nosson where he described the day Reb Nachman left the world:

Reb Nachman had tuberculosis. He was so sick. It was as if his soul was slowly, slowly leaving his body. He came to the point where he was just at the end. When Reb Nachman realized this, he began saying, "*Shema Yisrael Hashem Elokeinu Hashem Echad*" — G-d is One.

Reb Nosson wrote, "I swear to you, at the moment that Reb Nachman left the world, he said '*Hashem Echad*, G-d is One' like it was the first time he said it in his whole life."

What a way to leave the world, saying "G-d is One" for the first time.

What happens to you when you say good-bye to someone you love very much?

At that moment, your love for that person is like the first time you ever saw them.

Have you ever left the Holy Wall?

That is when we, so to speak, say good-bye to the Holy Temple. Can you imagine how much we love the Temple at that moment, how much we love G-d, how much G-d loves us?

So it is on Tisha b'Av that Mashiach is born, at the moment of utmost love.

⁂

All the Chassidish Rebbes say something so strong: When you see someone kissing a baby, can you be sure that the person is the child's father? Everybody likes to kiss a cute baby, so you can't be sure just from this who the father is.

But when you see someone spanking a baby, it has to be the father — because if it was someone else — well, who are you to spank my baby?

It is the same thing with G-d. When the Ribbono Shel Olam is good to us, maybe it just means He likes us. But when, G-d forbid, G-d has to knock us down a little bit — that is when we know that G-d is our Father.

It gets even deeper.

There are two types of fathers. I can walk into a house and see a father giving a *zetz* to his child. But it doesn't seem that it hurts him to spank his baby. He just does it. A lot of parents are like this.

Or, I can see another father giving a *zetz* to his baby, and the father is *mamesh* crying the whole time. While he is spanking his child, he is telling the kid, "I hope you know how much it hurts me to have to spank you."

Do you think G-d wasn't crying when He had to destroy the Holy Temple? Do you think it didn't hurt Him so much?

We don't learn what kind of Father the Ribbono Shel Olam is from the good things He does for us. We learn this from the *churban Beis Hamikdash*... from the destruction of the Holy Temple.

❦

Let's say my wife is angry at me. I knock on her door, and she yells from behind the door, "Go away! I don't want to see you."

If I don't really care about her, then I'll say, "Okay, if you don't want to see me, I'll just go marry somebody else."

But if I love her so, so much, I won't just go away. I can't leave. I'll put my ear very close to the door. Do you know what I'll hear? I'll hear her crying on the other side.

Do you know what was happening when G-d drove us out of the Holy Land? G-d said, "Get out of My land. Get out of My Holy Temple."

But even today, if we put our ears very close to the Holy Wall, we can still hear the Ribbono Shel Olam crying on the other side....

I once saw one of the most heartbreaking scenes I have ever seen in my life.

I had to be the third Rabbi for a *get,* a divorce.

It so happened, I was in a certain city, and they needed three rabbis together who were able to write the *get*. They had two rabbis and they *mamesh* needed one more.

The whole thing was like this, it was very obvious. On the level of wanting, this couple wanted to get divorced. On the level of *churban Hamikdash*, they *mamesh* didn't want it. It's crazy to say this, because it's not that they didn't want to get divorced. They did want to get divorced. But you know what they wanted to do? Somehow they wanted to be divorced, but they wanted a miracle to happen that everything would be good again, and they wouldn't need to be divorced. Meaning to say, the way it is now, they knew that they needed to get divorced, but they were waiting for a miracle. They wanted to wake up the next morning and everything would have been a nightmare.

So I said to the two rabbis, "We've got to talk to them on a different level, maybe we can get through to them." But I was just invited as a guest, I couldn't say much. After the husband gave his wife the *get*, he walked out of the room first. I saw him walk straight up to a tree that was under the window of the rabbi, and he was leaning his head against the tree, crying like a baby. Unbelievable. Five minutes later, the woman walked out. She walked straight to the same place. They were crying so much. I said to the rabbis "You know something, I don't want to swear but it looks to me that they are really meant for each other...."

What was going on with the destruction of the Holy Temple?

G-d says "Okay, get out of here, I want to divorce you."

Yet we find ourselves crying together with the Ribbono Shel Olam. G-d is crying and we are crying.

Secrets are such a delicate thing.

Not just secrets between people. But between G-d and people.

The Ribbono Shel Olam is so Holy that whenever you want to tell someone a secret and G-d feels it's not right, He gives you a sign, He tells you not to — because He is the greatest keeper of secrets.

Sometimes, you listen to His sign. But sometimes, you and I know the sad truth. You want to tell someone a secret and it just doesn't go. So you try again, "I've got to tell them." You force your way, you break the doors open and you tell them the secret. But it's not flowing. It wasn't meant to be.

What does mazel tov mean? *Mazel* means to flow, like the word "*nozel*." It means that everything should flow through. If you have to force something, it's a bad scene. You weren't supposed to tell the secret.

Think about it: What do you need a house for? You need a house to tell secrets. You don't tell secrets on the street. If I meet somebody I love and I want to tell them a secret I don't say "Meet me at the corner of 5th Avenue and 68th street." I will say "Come to my house." At my house, I can tell secrets. My secret is safe.

What does it mean to be in exile? It means that G-d has no secrets with me. As long has G-d has a secret with me, He needed a house to meet. The moment the house is destroyed, the Ribbono Shel Olam says "Listen, I love you, but there is no place that we can be alone. No secrets."

People who are in exile have no secrets. A broken down house means there are no secrets in the house anymore. And if there are no secrets, who needs a house? You can go live on the street.

That's us. We're homeless. After 2,000 years, we're still homeless. Still wandering. G-d's house is still destroyed. He can't tell us secrets in the street.

G-d has been waiting there the whole time, just to share these secrets with us once again.

There are many kinds of secrets.

Eichah, the Book of Lamentations, is written in accordance with the *alef beis*, sometimes it goes *alef*, *beis*, then it might go three *alefs*, three *beis'*, three *gimmels*, everything has to do with the letters. This has millions of reasons.

According to Kabbalistic tradition, a word is called a house, *teivah*. G-d might have taken the physical house from us, but He never took away the letters which compose the house. We are rebuilding the house with the letters.

Imagine a husband and wife that love each other very much. They have secret signs between them.

Imagine that something happens and he speaks only English and she speaks only French. They can't talk to each other on a language level. But they remember that they had secret signs between each other.

Do you know what this means?

The lowest Jew in the world, who forgot G-d's language, you know what is reaching them? G-d's secret signs, those unbelievable signs. In secret signs, you can say more than all the languages together.

Words come from the mind. The mind is good, but it is limited. Words are limited, they are finite.

Secret signs go from soul to soul. They have nothing to do with the mind. So even when the house is destroyed, the mind is destroyed, but the inside of the soul is untouched. If you still remember these secret signs, you can rebuild the House of G-d.

We are broken about G-d's broken House. We don't have the words.

But we still feel that there is a place deep inside of us which can never be destroyed, which is the greatest, most deepest sign in the world.

What's Yerushalayim *Ir Hakodesh* all about?

It's all about what took place in the Beis Hamikdash.

What did Aharon HaKohen tell the *Yiddele*, the lowest sinner who comes to Yerushalayim? The same question can be asked about what takes place to a person when they come to the Holy Wall? Why is it that when you are standing by the Holy Wall, suddenly you are a different *Yiddele*?

Before, you felt so far. You felt forgotten. Suddenly, from that moment on, you have secrets with G-d! The most intimate, beautiful secrets. Every *Yiddele* who stood by the Holy Wall for one moment, suddenly they had the deepest relationship to G-d. "*Sod Hashem lire'iav*," — "G-d's secrets are to those who fear Him."[39]

It was all secrets.

---

39   Tehillim 25:14

❦

Why is Mashiach born on Tisha b'Av? On the day that I lost everything, when I reach bottom, this is the time when I "get it." Because I realize I can't live without it anymore.

What's the difference between a hotel and a home?

You only live in a hotel when you're there. The home is the place that, even if you're not there, it gives you life.

A home gives you life. The Gemara says a person who has no home has no life.[40] They're dead.

Why is that? What's a house?

Everybody has books. There are books you are connected to when you read them. After you read them, you throw them out. You return them to the library. You forget all about it.

Imagine there's a book that you read once, but then didn't read it again for ten years. Then you see the book and you just look at it. You remember, *oy,* when I read it, it's so special. You know that you are connected to that book.

Now listen to this deepest depths.

G-d gives the Torah via our teacher, Moshe Rabbeinu.

The Holy Land, He gave through our fathers.

What is the difference between a father and a *rebbe*? It's very simple. I'm only connected to my teacher while I am learning. If I'm sitting in a class and I'm not learning one word, he's not really my teacher. He might be a good friend, he may be a nice guy, and he may let me pass, but he's not my teacher. If I'm not learning anything from him, he's not my teacher and I'm not his student.

On the other hand, my father is my father if I learn something or not. If I listen to him, or, G-d forbid, if not. I can do everything wrong but he's always my father.

The month that we were driven out of the Holy Land is called *chodesh* Av, the "month of the father."

---

40   Tractate *Yevamos* 63a

Why?

G-d revealed Himself to us three times. When G-d took us out from Egypt He revealed to us that He is G-d; "*Ani Hashem, Ani Hu v'lo acher.*"[41] We knew there was one G-d. It was the highest revelation there is on a G-d level. On Mount Sinai, G-d revealed Himself to us as a teacher. He taught us everything there is to know.

Do you know when G-d became our Father? In Eretz Yisrael. In Yerushalayim, the Holy City.

Even more — in His Home.

Even deeper: The utmost revelation that G-d is our Father was not when the Holy Temple was there — but when the Holy Temple was destroyed. Because it wasn't a hotel. It was a home.

According to our tradition, whenever a word is mentioned for the first time in the Bible, this is the headquarters for that word. This is what tells us how to understand what the word really means.

When is the first time in the Bible that somebody calls his father "father"?

It's unbelievable. When Yitzchak walked up with Avraham to the *akeidah* to be sacrificed, Yitzchak says to Avraham, his father, "*Vayomer Yitzchak el Avraham aviv, Vayomer avi vayomer hineni B'ni.*" "And he (Yitzchak) says my Father, And he (Avraham) said here I am, son."[42]

Do you know what this means. This is deeper than life. Do you know when Yitzchak *really knew* that Avraham was his father? When he was taken up to be sacrificed.

Do you know when we *really knew* that G-d is our Father? When He took us out of Yerushalayim to be sacrificed. The month of Av is called *av*, father, because that is when we realized that He is really our father. We lived in His House. Even today, we are still connected to His House.

What connects me to my *rebbe* is his teachings. If I can't remember what he taught, is he my *rebbe*? Someone asks me, what did your

---

41 Haggadah of Pesach
42 Bereishis 22:7

father tell you in your life? "It's a secret. I don't want to tell you." If I can easily share with you all which my father told me, it was not so deep. It is public, not private.

What's the highest connection between parents and children? Secrets. They tell each other things that they won't tell anyone else.

What is a home? A home is a place which is filled with secrets. It gives me life even when I'm not there. It isn't just a place. It has a soul. And it is filled with secrets.

When the Holy Apter visited Reb Shmelke's house 100 years later, he felt something beyond himself as soon as he walked in. He said that he could still smell the secrets. The holiest secrets.

On the outside, things look bad. G-d's home is broken. His People are crying. His People are in mourning.

But, if you have a good nose, you can smell the secrets. The secret is that we're still in His home. The secret is that Mashiach is coming.

The deepest secret in the world is not that G-d took us out of Egypt. Everybody knows that.

The deepest secret in the world is that G-d never left us. He is bringing us back to Yerushalayim. That is the deepest secret in the world.

It is possible to do everything G-d wants us to do, and still not be intimate with G-d. Mount Sinai was where G-d told us what to do, but Yerushalayim and the Beis Hamikdash were the headquarters of being close to G-d — and to each other. When the House was destroyed, there was no place to be intimate anymore. And *gevalt* are we longing and crying to be intimate with G-d again — shedding so many tears and begging G-d for intimacy with every Jew, with every word of the Torah, with every human being, with all of nature, and — one day — with the whole world.

Until we came back to Yerushalayim, we only heard the sound of destruction on Tisha b'Av, but we could not hear the footsteps of

Mashiach. Today the voice of destruction gets further and further away, and the voice of the coming of Mashiach gets closer and closer.

If you have good eyes, you can see that G-d never left. He is still in His House. He is still in Yerushalayim. He is still with us.

5. The Heart of Jerusalem

Do you know what Amalek said when we crossed the Red Sea? Amalek came up and he said that we Jews drowned the Egyptians and he made a commission to find out how come the Egyptians were drowned.

I'm sure there must have been Dasan and Aviram, two Jews with no character, on that commission.

Let's get back on our feet. Let's have some pride — some holy pride. I have pride in my People. We don't kill and we don't steal! We are the holiest People in the whole world!

When Mashiach comes, should he go to Washington? Rome? Berlin? Mashiach has only one People and one place.

We're the People and Yerushalayim *Ir Hakodesh* is the place.

There is no one else, and no other place.

Jerusalem is Mashiach's place and G-d's place.

Do you know how Yiddishkeit began?

Not with Mount Sinai. Yiddishkeit began with Avraham Avinu coming to the Holy Land. Everything is always directed toward Eretz Yisrael.

Imagine that there is a land where nothing was ever built. I can take a good architect there and say, "Can you build me a good house here?" So he makes some plans and builds me a beautiful house.

Now imagine that I take this architect to a place where there is what looks like the ruins of a destroyed house. And I say to him, "Brother, I don't want you to wipe out the ruins; I want what is left of the house to stay the way it is. And at the same time, I want you to rebuild the house in such a way that nobody can see that it was ever broken." Only G-d can do that.

Imagine that I love my wife very much, but we had a fight. Then someone else comes up to console me. It's possible. I'm consoled — mazel tov.

But it's not real; it's a cover-up. The only one who can really console me is my wife.

It's the same way with the Holy Temple. It has to be the same Beis Hamikdash. It cannot be a new one. It cannot be another land... it has to be Eretz Yisrael. It cannot be anything else...

Let's learn a little bit from Reb Ahron Karliner.

Physically, a person lives in a house and walks on the street.

Even while you are on the street, you never forget where you live. Deep down in your heart, you're always thinking about when you are going back.

It is the same thing, he explains, when you talk about anything which has to do with this world, since you really have to know that you are not from this world. Here, you are really only on the streets so to speak, but your home is really somewhere else. Even in your thoughts, you always have to think, *When am I going back?*

A lot of people are very *frum*. They are very sweet and very cute and are very holy. But, the question is: Where do you *mamesh* live, where does your *neshamah* live? How long can you stay away?

Let's say, for instance, if I leave my house, I can be gone for a few minutes without announcing it. If I walk away for a long time, I have to tell my wife I am leaving.

You can take off from deep things and holy things for a little while, but the question is — does it need an announcement? If you can walk away and get lost somewhere, that means that spiritually you don't have a home yet, it means you don't live anywhere yet.

When you walk on the street, you don't take everything with you. When you move, you change your address. It might be only one inch away, maybe in another apartment in the same house, but you are somewhere else now. So a person has to always be on these two levels. Where are you? Where is your home? How long are you away for?

On one level, a person has to keep on walking. You have to keep on moving, not to be in the same place as yesterday. Still, in a very holy way, we also must have a house that you don't move away from. There has to be a certain place where this is *mamesh* where I live. I can't get away for a long time.

Imagine Shabbos: I can walk on the street and someone tells me stupid jokes, but then I'm itching already... I've got to get back to Shabbos. If you can stay away from Shabbos too long that means my house is not so full of Shabbos.

When it comes to learning, this is so important. How long can you stay away from learning? If you can stay away for a long time, then you were never really there.

So what Reb Ahron Karliner is saying is that a person has to know exactly where he is living. Where do you live, spiritually? Where is your home? Even while you are away, don't stay away too long and always remember that you've got to go back.

Why is it so hard for some people to do *teshuvah*, and for other people it's not so hard? Very simple.

People who had a house even for one minute... you can go back, you know where you live. Even if I stay away from home for a long time, I can go back. A person who never had a home, who never had a spiritual home, where should he go to? What does *teshuvah* mean to him?

Hachnassas orchim, welcoming guests to your home is so incredibly important. Do you know what it means to take somebody into your house? The greatest mitzvah in the world is to invite someone into your house. It is spiritual, not just physical. I can give my life to somebody else, somebody who has no address, who has no home. I invite them to my house and suddenly, they will feel so much at home.

Imagine someone comes to Yerushalayim and he has nowhere to stay. Invite him to your house. Then deep down, even while they are walking down the street they have a feeling of "You know something, I have to go back to my house." They were only invited, but it's still very strong.

I want you to know something very, very strong:

There are two ways of learning. I can teach somebody something or, on the deepest level, I teach somebody on the level of inviting them to my house. This is so deep because the difference is very simple. If it's just on the level of teaching, then when you walk out — you have nothing to come back to. But if it was on the level of inviting you to my house, to where I stand in learning, you feel so much at home there. It becomes part of you, part of your home. So even if you get lost for a little bit you can always come back.

Do you know what Eretz Yisrael is? The holiness is that it's *mamesh* G-d's house. Yerushalayim is His house. *Mamesh!*

Even more: He made it our house as well.

G-d made it so much our house that we can be away for 2,000 years and we still know to go back.

Imagine if, for 2,000 years, a *Yiddele* wouldn't open a book, wouldn't keep Shabbos, and suddenly he feels that he has to go back to Shabbos, has to learn the book...

That is the power of the Holy Land... it is our house. We never really get lost. We always go back to it.

The difference between Mount Sinai and Eretz Yisrael is very simple. On Mount Sinai, G-d gave us the Torah, but we quickly got lost and made a golden calf.

From Eretz Yisrael, you can't get lost because it's a house. The teaching of Yerushalayim is on the level of a house. It is our house. Our only house.

How long can we be away from it?

❧

There is something so deep inside each of us.

Even while I'm thinking 2 million other things, deep inside, I'm thinking about something specific. Something which touches my heart very deep. You can ask me which restaurant I love the most and I'll answer you clearly, but there is a certain part of me, inside, which is always reserved.

Let's go one step deeper. My dreams do not depend on my *machshavah*, my conscious thought. My dreams depend on my *hirhur*.

Hirhur is that thought which takes place deep inside — a kind of thought which you might not even be aware of thinking it. I can talk to someone for two hours, I think that I'm not even thinking about it… but I am.

This kind of thinking is between conscious and unconscious. It's not consciousness but it's also not unconsciousness. It is unique.

Yerushalayim is the one place I never stop thinking about.

You can talk to me about anything in the world, but deep, deep inside, I'm thinking about Yerushalayim.

You can talk to me about anything in the world, but deep, deep inside, I don't stop thinking about the 6 million. I can't.

How can you forget them for one second?

How can you forget Yerushalayim for one second?

❧

Everything in the world has a headquarters.

Every person is chosen for something special.

Every nation is chosen for something special.

There is the headquarters for this "chosenness," where everyone goes to find out for what he or she is chosen for.

The headquarters for "chosenness" is the Holy City.

When you come to the Holy City to pray, you know that G-d has chosen you, just you, for something so special.

◈

How do you connect one human being with the other? With our hands. Words are very beautiful, but my words can be for something or can be against something.

Holding hands with another human being is the deepest connection. When people love each other, what do they do? They hold hands all the time. When little children are born, you carry them with your hands.

Today there is a big hurricane. Everyone is talking about building memorials for the 6 million, you know what they are talking about? Against evil, against cruelty, against the Germans. Against, against, and against. How about teaching our children to connect themselves to those 6 million by telling them who they were? Do you know what our children are tired of? They are tired of us telling them this one killed us, this one wants to kill us, this one could have killed us, and this one might kill us.

That is all we are about?

We are the Chosen People to talk about killers?

No wonder our children can't stand us.

Once, a young lady told me "I'm sick and tired of sob stories. That's all my father or mother tells me. They tell me that my grandfather was in this pogrom and my great-grandfather was in another pogrom. When they talk about Israel, all they talk about are the wars."

Is this what makes me into a Jew? Do you think that I will bring peace to the world by telling my children about all the pain we went through for thousands of years?

We need a deeper kind of learning, a much deeper kind of learning.

You have to learn the deepest depths of the Torah. You know why we are so against? Because our insides are empty, our hearts are empty, our ideas are so empty that any wind can blow away all the ideas of the world. Do you know why our children are leaving us? Because their souls are hungry. Have you ever walked the streets of the world? People are so hungry.

This is our generation, it's you and I, but most of all it's our children. There is such a hunger in the world, a hunger for something beautiful and holy. A hunger for one good word, for a message from G-d.

People who are hungry for bread hate each other. People who are hungry for something lofty and glorious love each other so much. Hungry people feel so close to each other.

Do you know what will bring peace to the world? Not the politicians, not the great businessmen, but little hungry people.

I have walked the streets of the world, I'm sure you have too. It is so clear — the world is hungry, the world is so hungry. Sometimes, people stop you on the street and they ask you for the time even though they have a watch. Do you know what they are telling you? Half my life is gone, I'm still hungry.

Sometimes, people ask you on the street "Where is the next street?" They are not idiots, they could find it if they wanted to. They are telling you "I don't know where to go. I have an address, I am a rich man and I have everything but I don't know where I'm going, maybe you have a message for me from G-d? Maybe you have a message for me from someone who loves me? Show me the way... show me the way to fill my heart, to fill my soul."

Yerushalayim, the Holy City, is headquarters for the hungry people. Someday, the hungry people of the world will get together and they will pray together, and this is what the prophet says. *"Va'havi'osim el har kodshi vesimachtim b'veis tefillasi oloseihem v'zivcheihem leratzon al mizbechi"* — "And I will bring them to My holy mountain. And I will make them glad in My House of Prayer. Their burnt offerings and their sin offerings a free will offering on My altar." Isaiah says *"Ki beisi beis tefillah yikare l'chol ha'amim."* —"For My House will be called a House of Prayer for all the nations."⁴³

Do you know what praying is? I pray for real when I need something on the level of hunger. I'm hungry… hungry for the greatest revelation.

༺⁂༻

There are different kinds of miracles. Some people think of the miracles of G-d: The Red Sea opens. G-d took us out of Egypt, it's the great miracle!

Yerushalayim is the headquarters for a different kind of miracle. When the sun shines in the morning, it's the greatest miracle in the world. When the moon is shining at night, it's the greatest miracle in the world. When little children are born, there is no greater miracle in the world. The first time a baby is crying is the biggest miracle in the world. The first time a baby is laughing, is the highest miracle in the world.

The headquarters for all this is Yerushalayim, the Holy City. Yerushalayim the Holy City. Some people think I have to pray to G-d if someone is sick. That is the kind of prayer you can do anywhere in the world.

Yerushalayim is deeper. Let me wake up in the morning, Almighty, give me strength to walk, Almighty give me strength to breathe. Give me strength to live in this Holy World.

Someday, the whole world will come to Yerushalayim and they will look at each other and will know that every human being is a miracle from the One, the Only One. Then there will be peace in the world, because how can you not love G-d's miracles?

Let me tell you, on the level of holidays, the headquarters for this kind of miracle — when everything is taking its natural way and that

---

43   Yishayahu 56:7

it's a miracle — is Purim. Purim is the holiday that nothing extraordinary happens, but everything is a miracle. When you get drunk with joy, not that G-d does a miracle which is out of the ordinary, but when you realize, "Ribbono Shel Olam, You created me, we are living, my children are alive," I am blowing my mind with joy.

It's a miracle! The fact that we are together is the greatest miracle in the world; that we are alive, we are singing and dancing. It's the greatest miracle in the world.

And it all starts in Yerushalayim. Yerushalayim is the headquarters of miracles.

❦

The world is composed of light and vessels.

An endless amount of light flows down from the heavens every day, the question is do you know how to bottle it? Do you know how to contain it? A lot of people walk around in this world and they're broken. A lot of people have a lot of lights, but they have no vessels for their own light. They don't have the vessels for their own light. They don't know what to do with it.

What do they do? Either they force their light into the little vessel that they have. Or they decide to lead a life of vessels and disregard the light. They have little vessels, and they have a little light.

Take most of the world today. They have a little light, little vessels. Everything is straight.

Or they decide to live on a "light-level." That means they have no vessels. They're broken all the time. Nothing. But it's also no good. Because the world is both light and vessels.

Imagine if I *mamesh* believe that I should walk on the streets every day and I should give gifts to everybody. That's my light. Or I should walk around giving gifts. I leave my wife, my children. I just walk around on the streets giving gifts. It's a very holy thought. It's a very holy light, but I'm ending up being crazy. All light, no vessels.

Or I think that *No, I can't because right now I have a job, I've got to support my wife and children*. Vessels I have, but I abandon the light. Either way is bad.

The world does not know yet the secret of light and vessels. They either have vessels or they have light. They don't know yet the secret of light within vessels. There's no one to teach them because for most people, it's all vessel talk.

The secret of Torah is that we have the light within vessels. The craziest thing about the words of the Torah is that those words are vessels for great light. A real holy teaching is not something that makes you crazy. A real holy teaching is that which makes your light deeper and your vessels stronger and bigger.

The Baal Shem Tov would always bless people that their body should be strong enough for their soul. Everybody can make themselves either crazy or make themselves shine like an atomic explosion. What's going to be with your body? A lot of people have a lot of light but no vessels. So what do you do? You want to be holy? Leave your wife and your children and go live like a monk. The Hare Krishna kids; they have a great light, but no vessels because this is not the world you're living in.

You don't walk around with a shaved head asking everybody for a penny. This isn't where it's at. What's wrong with standing in a grocery store and selling herring? It's very holy if I know how to sell it. But this is a hidden kind of holiness.

Sure, if I'm standing and praying, it's very holy. But to sell herring or to be a mailman can be even holier. It's a very holy thing to bring somebody a letter. It can be the most holy thing in the world. Do you know what it means to deliver somebody a letter? *Gevalt*, I can work for the post office and say it's really bad, or I can do it thinking that it's the greatest privilege in the world to bring somebody a message. It might change their whole life. Whatever you do, you can do it on the highest level or the lowest level. It depends if your vessels and your light is strong.

The whole world is full of light, but Yerushalayim is a vessel for this holy light. Every house could be a Holy Temple, but it isn't because they have no vessel. How can a house be a vessel if it's not a house?

Yerushalayim is the place that this holy little house is a vessel for this light. Everybody can be a High Priest. Aharon HaKohen was the one who made vessels for it. Moshe Rabbeinu was the one who had strong enough vessels to go on Mount Sinai, talk to G-d, and come back to tell us. If I would have a revelation like Moshe Rabbeinu did, where I *mamesh* hear G-d talking to me... I'd crack up completely. Moshe Rabbeinu can. Can you imagine? It's not only that his light was holy, he had real strong vessels for his light.

The Alter Rebbe and Reb Avraham HaMalach were sitting and learning one night. Heaven and earth opened up before them. During the awesome learning, the Alter Rebbe went into the kitchen to get a bagel. And he even remembered to put butter on the bagel. Imagine what a cool vessel he was. He didn't forget to put butter on because this is the way of the world. His vessels were strong. He wasn't one ounce less holy than when he had the revelation. He was completely with it.

Today, what we have to do very strong is not only have holy lights, we also must have very holy vessels.

I'll tell you something very, very strong. A lot of times, people love each other from afar. That means the great light is shining. But when it comes to meeting each other, they have no vessels. They don't even say hello to each other. Have you ever seen this? Sometimes there is someone you love who you really want to see, but then you're standing in front of them and you don't know what to say because you have no vessels. Sometimes, I want to tell someone I love them. The light is so strong. But I don't know how to say it. I have no vessels.

Or, sometimes, I say that I love you, but its vessels have no light, so it's also meaningless.

The secret of the world is light and vessels.

Yerushalayim is headquarters of finding our light and our vessels.

In Chassidus, there is such a thing as *Olam hatikun v'olam hatohu*. *Olam hatohu* means a chaos world. What's chaos? Everything is there but not in their right places. Imagine you take the house you're living in and turn it over. Turn over all the furniture. Put the dishes in the bed, the bed in the refrigerator. And someone will say, "Hey, is anything missing?" "No, everything is here." You can't live like this because the light and the vessels don't mix. We're all over the place. What we are here for is to figure out where things belong because everything has its proper place.

Yerushalayim is the headquarters of everything having its proper place.

Yerushalayim is the headquarters of everyone finding their place. Of finding their light and letting it shine in its right place — their vessels.

Do you think any human being is actually bringing any peace to the world?

Reading the newspapers, it seems that this one wants peace, this one doesn't want peace… do you think that the other one will bring peace? They won't.

It's He, the Only One, the One that created the world, and if we would only be deserving, if we could only be on such a high level to receive the holiness of peace, there would be peace in the world. At that very moment, there will be peace in the world.

I want to tell you something very beautiful. In Hebrew, the word *ir* — which is spelled with the holy letters *ayin, yud, reish* — means city.

It also means to wake up — *lehit'orer* — the root word is the same.

Yerushalayim is called *Ir Hakodesh*, the Holy City. But it really means the city which wakes up all that which is holy within you. When you come to Yerushalayim, you have to wake up.

And it goes even deeper. Yerushalayim wakes up the world. It is the center of the world and it wakes up the whole world.

Waking up the world to what real peace is.

Waking up the world to feel and experience G-d in the most real way.

❧

The holiest thing about human beings is that we are created in G-d's image and we have choice. Each time I choose something, maybe I'm doing the wrong thing, but I am using my free choice.

So many people are hungry for slavery because it's frightening to have free choice. For certain people, religion is really like a way back to slavery — I don't have to choose. I get myself a little book, G-d's "yellow pages," and every morning I look up what I am supposed to do; and if I don't know the page, I'll pray like mad, "G-d, show me the page," and I tune in and I hear G-d's voice, clearly. This isn't what G-d's religion is all about, but what some people do to religion.

On the one hand, I have to know that if I choose wrong, I really lose. It's very important to know the responsibility of choosing. If a person doesn't feel the responsibility of choosing, then they are not human beings.

And here I want to share with you the deepest depths.

Do you know what it means to really love somebody? To really love somebody means that it's beyond choice. Even if you make every wrong choice in your whole life, I still love you the same. Love is beyond choice.

A house, also, is a place where my being has nothing to do with choice. It is deeper than choice. That means that a house is a place where, even if I choose everything wrong, the door is still open. Anything that has to do with choice is on the street; my house is deeper than choice.

Do you know where I feel at home? In a place which has nothing to do with choice. Imagine a place where I always have to make excuses why I do this, why I do that. You don't like it anymore because you feel like you are on the street.

The responsibility of choice I learn on the street. A home, a house, a House of G-d is not about choice. Choice is irrelevant.

In the Holy Temple, a person comes and stands before G-d and says to G-d, "You know, I made the wrong choice." Aharon HaKohen, the High Priest, comes and says, "You know what, it's okay, you're still okay."

Moshe Rabbeinu is the one who taught us the awesomeness of choice. The holiness of what took place on Mount Sinai is the awesomeness of choice.

Yerushalayim, the Holy City, the City of G-d is the place where even if you choose wrong — G-d still loves you. It'll be okay. It already is.

Mount Sinai will not turn on the world to G-d because not everybody wants the awesomeness of free choice.

Eventually, the world will realize that even with all the bad choices we made, we're still okay with G-d. Then it says some day the Holy Temple will be a House of Prayer to the whole world; a house.

The Temple is our house. Our only house. Completely different than the street.

⁂

Do you know what the problem of our generation is? We don't know the depths of our own souls. We don't know the depths of our own foundation. We are living in a world with so much perversion. Some of today's kids are *mamesh* so holy, but they are also a little bit off. What is their problem? Their houses are destroyed, they don't have a foundation.

So when your house is broken, you rebuild the four walls. It might seem like you are fixing your house but that at the same time, you are shutting out everyone else. Reb Leibe'le Eiger says that's not true. Do you know what you are really doing? Not only are you fixing your house — you really are fixing the whole world.

You know friends, people who love one person completely are not capable of hating. They simply can't hate anyone in the world. When you say that you love the whole world, you can still hate someone. But when you love one person completely — you can't hate because this one person becomes your Holy Temple. And from this Holy Temple your love for the whole world is shining.

All the Rebbes say that every one of us must have one *masechta*, one section of the Gemara that we love the most. Even in relation to the Torah, we need one *masechta*, one page, which is the foundation for the rest of the Torah.

When you absolutely love one person — it becomes your foundation for all the love in the world.

Yerushalayim, the Holy City, teaches us to fix our foundation, to focus on what we love the most and continue from there.

There are two worlds of Torah. There is the Torah of Mount Sinai, which you learn, and there is the Torah of the Holy Land, which you only learn by mistake. Can you imagine on what level G-d wants to give it to us. We've been making mistakes for so long...

"*Im eshkachech Yerushalayim tishkach yemini*"[44] — We can't forget Yerushalayim. Can't forget.

There are Jews who can forget they are Jews but they cannot forget the Holy Land. Someone might pretend that he can. You and I, we know hundreds of thousands of people. When there was the Six Day War, the lowest creepiest Jew was with it all the way. We didn't take advantage of it. All the Jews would have come to Israel the next day if we had pushed.

---

44   Tehillim 137:5

I know a *Yiddele*, a very rich man from Los Angeles, who had thousands and thousands in the bank. He would go to shul once a year, on Yom Kippur night. That's it.

During the Six Day War, he took all the money from his bank and sent it to Israel. Today this *Yiddele* is living in Israel, he wears *tzitzis*, he has a beard. He was one of the Jews that gave his whole heart and G-d rewarded him for it.

Yom Kippur didn't touch him. Yiddishkeit didn't touch him. Nothing touched him.

Except for Yerushalayim. Yerushalayim touched him.

He knew it was the center, the heart, the headquarters... of everything.

There are two ways of learning something in the deepest depths.

Imagine I finally meet my soul mate. It goes fast and, mazel tov, four weeks later we're married. Does it blow your mind?

Now imagine that the same thing happens, but before the marriage we somehow lose track of each other. We *mamesh* can't locate each other.

Do you know something? For 2,000 years, I do everything I can to find her. One day, *gevalt*, I find her. Do you know how deep this is?

Do you think it is the same marriage as the first one? No, it is something else.

We love Yerushalayim so much that we've been searching for it for 2,000 years.

We love Yerushalayim so much *because* we've been searching for it for 2,000 years.

Mount Sinai is the straight teachings: Four corner *tzitzis*, don't eat ham. Everything is straight learning. Very important, very holy but the way I learn about it is by learning what is written about it.

Yerushalayim is the city of mistakes. Everything is mistakes. Do you know why King David is the one who built Yerushalayim?

King David is the master of mistakes. He made lots of mistakes, but he never gave up. *Dovid melech Yisrael chai v'kayam*, he lives forever. There is no mistake in the world big enough for him to give up.

Why is it that right after Shabbos we have the feast of King David?

Because I know I'm going to make 2 million mistakes this week. So King David gives me strength.

So what, you made a mistake, so what?

Yerushalayim is the headquarters of mistakes — and the headquarters of the world, and of G-d.

Reb Nachman says that there are two levels of connecting to G-d, *emes* and *emunah* — Truth and Faith.[45]

Mount Sinai is the headquarters for the truth.

Yerushalayim, the Holy City, is the headquarters of faith, of believing.

In the whole world, outside Israel, I can know G-d. I can know, no matter where I am in the world, that there is One G-d. This is on the level of truth.

The revelation of G-d in the Holy Land is a completely different level. It's on the level of believing.

On Mount Sinai, I saw that there is One G-d. G-d revealed Himself to me. He came down on Mount Sinai. I saw lightning and thunder, and I heard G-d's Voice. It was clear to me like daylight.

What happens to you now when you walk down the streets in Yerushalayim? You see a little Wall… it's something else.

So here Reb Nachman begins to say that there is such a thing as *davening with* my nature and there is such a thing as *davening beyond* my nature. Beyond nature, your beyond nature, depends on how much you believe. This is your level of beyond nature.

Praying doesn't mean those five minutes you're standing and

---

45 *Likutei Moharan* 7

praying. King David says *"V'ani tefillah"* — "I am a prayer."[46]

The people who daven, who pray for two minutes, mumble words, so they utter a prayer. It's sweet — but it's nothing.

The question is, are you a prayer? Are you filled with prayer? If you're filled with prayer, it means that you are beyond nature.

To be a prayer means that you believe in everything in the world. I can see a person who's the lowest person and I believe that this person can be brought up to the highest level. I can sit in Auschwitz and they can tell me tomorrow morning there will be no Jews left in the whole world. And I believe that we'll go right back to Yerushalayim and build the Holy Temple.

It's crazy.

Reb Nachman says that Israel, the Holy Land, is the headquarters for miracles. Because everybody knows that your level of miracles depends on how much you are connected to prayers. You see, if a person tells you "I don't believe in miracles," you know what that means? That this person has never prayed in his life, simple as it is.

Reb Nachman asks: What does it mean to be in exile?

Israel is the headquarters for prayer, the headquarters for miracles, the headquarters for completely believing in a relationship with G-d.

In exile, we don't know how to pray, because, obviously, the Holy Temple is the headquarters for praying.

Israel is the Land of prayers and the Holy Temple is the headquarters and the essence of the Holy Land. Since the Holy Temple is destroyed, that means our prayers are destroyed.

You know what it is to be in exile? To be in exile is that we have trouble believing that there is something beyond nature, beyond everything — and that everything is possible. The world is full of mistakes. I am full of mistakes. Nothing is clear. Nothing good seems possible.

Yerushalayim reminds me that good things are possible. Everything is possible.

---

46 Tehillim 109:4

The Gemara asks why the Beis Hamikdash was destroyed, and answers, "*Shelo birchu baTorah techilah*."[47] When they were learning Torah, they didn't bless G-d before they would learn. They were learning Torah, but it's possible to learn about G-d and forget that there is one G-d in the world. It's possible.

The Chozeh of Lublin would sit next to Reb Shmelke while Reb Shmelke would learn. Every six or seven or eight minutes, he was supposed to give him a *shuckle* on his sleeve and say there is one G-d, just to remind him.

Reb Shmelke was learning G-d's words. Do you know on what level Reb Shmelke's learning was, and yet, he was learning everything G-d says and it was still possible to forget there was one G-d. The Seer of Lublin says it never happened that he had to remind him that there was one G-d. But he said, "One time, so he was so deep in thought so I thought maybe I should give him a little *schuckle* on his sleeve to remind him there is one G-d and I was just about to put my hand on his sleeve and he said to me 'Ya'akov Yitzchak, it's okay, I remember'."

He didn't forget, but we do. We can learn G-d's Torah and forget G-d. Between people it's so true also: It's possible to love another person so much and yet absolutely forget the other person. Some parents love their children so much but they don't even remember their children. Sounds impossible? It is the story of our generation.

What do you remember?

Who have you forgotten?

If you meet a new person and you'd like to know who they are, it's very simple.

The first question I ask them is, "What makes you happy?" If the

---

47 Tractate *Bava Metzia* 85b

person will answer you, "More money in my bank," you know with whom you are talking.

On Shabbos, we say, "*Samcheinu Hashem Elokeinu, b'Eliyahu Ha-Navi, U'bemalchus beis David.*" "Make us happy the Lord our G-d with Elijah the Prophet and with the Kingdom of David."[48] The only thing which will ever really make me happy is if there will be peace in the world, if the world will be the way it should be.

Until Eliyahu comes, nothing will do. If I ask someone, which country are you a citizen of? They start telling me, I'm a citizen of this country, of that country. I'll ask, who is your king, who is your president? They tell me.

Do you know what I say? "*U'bemalchus beis David, Meshichecha.*" The Kingdom of King David. I'm a subject of King David, he is still my king, I don't know anybody else.

We're not looking for money or power. That won't make us happy. That's not who we are. We want King David. He is my king. He will always be my king, He will be my king to the end of all generations… Then we say, *B'meheirah yavo*, Let him come, the great king of the world, the great Messiah, true Messiah, *B'meheirah, yavo*.

Then we say, You promised us, Your Light will burn forever. Let there be no wind in the world that can blow this holy fire out.

"*Ki b'shem kadshecha, nishbata lo, shelo yichabeh nero, l'olam va'ed.*"[49]

"In Your Holy Name, I promise you, the candles will never go out."

In Riminov by the Holy Reb Hershele, the windows were open Friday night and the windows were lined with little candles, *Shabbosdik* candles.

One Friday night there was a storm and the *shames* said to the

---

48   Blessing after the Haftara
49   ibid

Riminover "I think we have to close the windows, because the wind will blow out the *Shabbosdik* candles."

The Riminover got very angry and said "How dare you say such an evil thing about the wind! Wait - I'll tell the wind."

The Holy Riminover walked to the window and he looked up at the sky and he said, "Wind, please wind, please don't blow out my *Shabbosdik* fire."

You know friends what we have to do.

The storm is still blowing.

The storm blew out 6 million *Shabbosdik* candles.

Do you know why Yerushalayim is the eternal city? Because for 2,000 years, we talked to the wind about Yerushalayim. We prayed: Holy wind, holy wind, take care of Yerushalayim, the Holy City. Holy wind, holy wind. Protect our children, holy wind, holy wind. Carry all my prayers to Yerushalayim. It is our heart. It is the heart of everything.

What is G-d doing all the time? G-d is praying.

When I'm learning, I can know. When I am praying, I can reach an even higher level. I can also hear G-d's praying.

How can you know if you are a little bit on the level to hear G-d pray? When you pray for somebody else.

If I pray for myself, it's my prayer, if I pray for somebody else, then I am reaching the level that I'm praying G-d's prayers. Imagine if someone is sick. What does G-d do? G-d prays to let them be well. If I am on the level of really praying for somebody else that means that, at that moment, I am on the level of hearing G-d's prayer.

I don't know exactly what this all means, but these words — to hear words like "G-d is praying" — it really cleanses the soul.

Sometimes, you hear good music and you're not sure who or what it is, but you know it sounds good.

Reb Nachman says like this, what is the whole creation about? All of creation is one thing, learning and praying. That's all there is, that's all there is to it. So "*Bereishis*," "In the beginning G-d created heaven and earth," if you really want to complete the creation of heaven and earth you have to know the secret of learning how to pray.

Do you know what the holiness of Yerushalayim is?

Yerushalayim is where G-d prays.

ص

The first Jew who went into exile being a slave is Yosef. Everybody knew by prophecy that eventually, us *Yiddelach* will be slaves. Do you know what Yosef was praying for his whole life? "Let me be the one to go through slavery instead of all my brothers. Don't put it on them, don't put it on my father." The Medrash says that Ya'akov was supposed to go down to Egypt in chains.[50] But Yosef took the whole thing of going down to Egypt in such shame — all on himself.

Why did Yosef tell his dreams to his brothers? Was it that he couldn't control himself? Was he a yenta? Was he *mamesh* in analysis and one of his brothers was a psychiatrist?

The answer is very simple, Yosef knew one thing. If I am supposed to be the slave and I want to take this upon myself, the saddest thing in the world is that I have to separate myself from my brothers and go by myself. So Yosef knew that the moment he tells these dreams to his brothers, they will be angry at him.

Do you see what's so crazy? Imagine you walk up to somebody and you tell them "I love you the most in the whole world," and they think *Ah, I know what you mean. You want to manipulate me, you want to take advantage of me.* When Yosef said "I'll be the king," what did he mean? He meant to say "I will take the whole burden for you."

And here you have to *mamesh* open your hearts. An unholy king is someone who really does take advantage. You work for me, you are my slave and I am the king.

---

50 *Bereishis Rabba* 86b

What is a holy king, what is a G-dly king? Not that you are working for him, but that he is working for you.

Let me ask you, sweetest friends. Everybody knows that Yerushalayim belongs to King David, it's his personal property. Why is Jerusalem King David's own property?

The answer is very simple. The seven nations who occupied all of Israel were such strong warriors, they were living on that hill where Yerushalayim is, and you couldn't get close. For 300 years after Yehoshua came into Israel, nobody conquered Yerushalayim. It was the heart of the people, the heart of everything, and we couldn't get to it.

Hoshana Raba, the seventh day of Succos, is the day of King David. Why is it his day? Do you know what happened on that Hoshana Raba? King David decided "I'm going to take Yerushalayim all by myself." One man, all by himself. If you trust G-d, does it matter to G-d if one man is going or a thousand people are going? It's the same thing.

On Hoshana Raba, King David walked up to Yerushalayim and he conquered the whole city. That is a king. A king is not someone who says "Listen folks, let's go, I want you to be killed. I am sitting here in my office, directing traffic." For that, you don't have to be King David.

Yerushalayim is David's city because he was a G-dly king. And Yerushalayim is G-d's city.

Imagine a homeless beggar would be roaming the streets of our neighborhood, and I would ask you "Could you maybe give this guy half a million dollars?" A normal human being would say "Really, a chutzpah. I just gave you $100,000 this morning and two hours later you bother me again?"

But let's assume that we are such good friends, who cares what I asked you for before? I'll give it to you. But imagine if I call him up a few hours later and I say, "Listen, this is for another *schlepper*, he needs a few thousand dollars." So he will say "Please brother, don't call me for another year, have compassion."

This is how a normal human being might respond, but you know the way G-d is? G-d gives me a little piece of cake, a little vegetarian dinner. So when I say the blessings after eating, I come to G-d and I say *"U'vnei Yerushalayim,"* can you please rebuild Yerushalayim, can you please bring the Mashiach? G-d says "What kind of chutzpah is this? Because I gave you a little bagel therefore you bother me right away about Yerushalayim?"

But now listen to the other side, I want you to open your hearts.

The test is what happens after doing a favor for a person. You could either think "Really, what a chutzpah, I just did you a favor, really… that's it, don't talk to me for another year."

If you love somebody very much, it's the other way around. If you do that one favor, you can't not do another favor. It is so beautiful to do someone a favor.

Imagine that my daughter will ask me for orange juice. Ten minutes later, she will say "I want more orange juice." I could say "A chutzpah."

Instead, I say, "I'm so glad to give you what you want." I am jumping out of my skin. Imagine ten minutes later she will say "Take me to Israel." I will blow my mind, she wants to go to Israel.

If I love someone, I want to give them more. And more.

When I say the blessing after a meal, I can have a little taste of how much G-d loves us, based on what I ask for. I eat one bagel, and say "Thank You for this bagel, but *'U'vnei Yerushalayim.* Please Ribbono Shel Olam, bring the Messiah, fix the whole world." He wants to give us. He wants to give us Yerushalayim. He wants to give us more and more.

❦

According to our tradition, there are thirty-six holy people in the world. They uphold the world. Sometimes, you wake up in the morning, you listen to the radio or you buy a newspaper and you think G-d is crazy.

For whom is He running this show? For whom does He keep this door open?

True, if the world would be the way you think it is. If this is all there is to the world, you are right. It looks crazy. Might as well shut the whole thing down.

But there are thirty-six holy people in the world. Just for them alone, the world keeps on going.

The streets of Yerushalayim have always been blessed with these thirty-six tzaddikim, walking its streets.

Here is a story from about 180 years ago. Everyone in the world has heard of the Kozhnitzer Maggid, the holy, the exalted, the deep, tremendous, may his memory be a blessing for all of Israel.

One day, the Rabbi of Czenslochov came to him, and he said, "Holy Rabbi, I've been married for eighteen years and G-d has not blessed us yet with children. Please holy Rebbe, holy master, pray for us. Bless us with children."

The Kozhnitzer Maggid closed his holy eyes, he said, "I'm so sorry, all the Heavens are closed." The Rabbi started to cry. He knew what it would be to leave the world without children. "Rebbe I can't believe that no one can open the gates of Heaven."

The Kozhnitzer Maggid said to him, "My dear Rabbi, do you know by any chance, in your city there is a *Yiddele* named Shvartze Wolf?"

"Shvartze Wolf? The most obnoxious Jew in the whole city. Disgusting, vulgar, no one wants to talk to him. Whenever he walks into shul, everyone walks away."

"Yes, that's him, he is the head of the thirty-six tzaddikim. In his hands are heaven and earth. If you can get invited by him for one Shabbos, he can bless you. He is the only one, the only one. For him, all the gates of Heaven are open."

Do you know what it means to go to one of the *lamed vav tzaddikim*, the holiest of holies, the deepest of the deep?

The Rabbi of Czenslochov came home. To prepare himself, he recited psalms, he repented, he promised G-d everything in the world.

Shvartze Wolf lives in the forest. He's a woodchopper. The Rabbi thought that the only way he can be invited for Shabbos is if he knocks on his door two minutes before Shabbos. I'll tell him I got lost in the forest and he'll have to invite me. So, two minutes before Shabbos, this Rabbi knocks on the door of Shvartze Wolf.

Think about this carefully. The *lamed vav tzaddikim* are so holy. They are absolutely your mirror.

If you look at them and they look obnoxious, it is because you are obnoxious.

If you look at them and they look ugly, *gevalt* are you ugly.

If you look at them and see how holy they are, it's because you are so holy!

The Rabbi of Czenslochov knocks on the door of Shvartze Wolf and the ugliest woman in the world comes to the door. She is obnoxious, with the most vulgar language, disgusting, cursing. She opens the door and curses him out!

He says, "Please invite me for Shabbos! I'm lost in the forest, I can't make it back to the city anymore."

Let me not tell you what she said!

He said, "Please, please, please," and she tried to slam the door in his face.

He's very fast, he put his foot in the door. He looks at the children, he never saw such obnoxious looking children. Usually, children look beautiful, but these kids look terrible. She says to him, "If my husband comes home, and he finds you here, you'll never see daylight again. He'll kill you with his own hands. The only thing I can suggest to you, if you must stay, you can stay in the stable. There's a horse there, do your own thing and don't dare open the door to our house." He had two candles and a little challah and fish.

The *lamed vav tzaddikim* have their own minyan. Late, late at night, Shvartze Wolf comes home and he knows someone is in the barn. The door opens. It was frightening! He looks gruesome. He walks up to the Rabbi and says, "If you dare open the door of my house, I'm killing you with my own hands. And one second after Shabbos I want you to disappear from my stable." He slams the door!

He couldn't sleep Friday night. Shvartze Wolf is next door. All he needs is one blessing. He can't go in, but he needs the blessing. Early Shabbos morning, he heard Shvartze Wolf go daven in the forest. Late afternoon he came back. He's trying to do *teshuvah*, Ribbono Shel Olam, I promise you! He begs, he pleads, he prays. There comes a point that he doesn't have anything more to say to G-d.

It's getting later and later and suddenly he looks out the window of the stable. There are three stars in the sky. Shabbos is over. It looks to me like I'll never have children. Then he remembered, there is one that can open the gates. There is Somebody so close — and yet so far — that can do everything! He fell to the ground and for the first time in his life he *mamesh* prayed to G-d, "Please let me have children!!"

At that moment, he felt the softest hand on his head. He looked up and saw Shvartze Wolf, shining like the High Priest on Yom Kippur. He said to him, my dearest sweetest friend, come in and join me for *melaveh malkah*. And whatever the Rabbi of Czenslochov thought the Beis Hamikdash would look like, believe me, the house of Shvartze Wolf was even more holy. And the wife of Shvartze Wolf who looked so ugly yesterday, she was so exquisitely beautiful. The children were all like High Priests. Shvartze Wolf said, "I know what you came for, and I bless you to have a son. I have only one request, call him Shvartze Wolf."

The Rabbi got the blessing from Shvartze Wolf!

The rabbi returns to the village. The next morning, there is a commotion in the synagogue. The *shammes* is walking around the synagogue asking everyone for a favor and nobody wants to do it. He asks the *shammes*, "What's going on here?"

"Someone died and nobody wants to go to the funeral."

"Who died?"

Shvartze Wolf. The holy of holiest, the deepest of the deep, the most precious of all precious.

The rabbi goes up to the *bimah* and yelled from the deepest depths of his being, "Do you know who he was? He was the head of the *lamed vav tzaddikim*! He was the holiest person of our generation. We never said good Shabbos to him, we never gave him an *aliyah*. We laughed at him...."

This was many years ago.

In 1944, the holy Rebbe of Belz came to the Holy Land.

His first Shabbos was in Tel Aviv. In Belz, everybody puts a bottle of wine and beer on the table, everybody gets a glass of wine. You walk up to the Rebbe and you tell him your name and your father's name or your mother's name, and the Rebbe blesses you.

There was a very old *Yiddele* and two people were holding him. He made his way to the Belzer Rebbe. The Belzer Rebbe says to him, "My *tier*, *zeisa* Yid, my precious brother, what is your name?"

He said, "My name is Shvartze Wolf."

The Belzer Rebbe says to him, "Are you the grandson of the first Shvartze Wolf who was called after the *lamed vav tzaddik*?"

"Rebbe, you know the story?"

The Belzer Rebbe says, "Yes, *heilege* Shvartze Wolf. I know the story, but nobody ever remembers, unless you do me a favor." He said, "Please lift up this *Yiddele*," maybe he was 100 years old. "Lift him up and sit him on the table. Let him tell all the Yidden here so the story should be remembered."

I had the privilege of hearing the story from a person who was at that first Friday night in Belz in Tel Aviv.

This is not the end. A number of years ago, I had the privilege of giving a concert in Ohel Shem in Tel Aviv, and out of nowhere I remembered the story of Shvartze Wolf and I told the people.

Suddenly, in the last row, someone began to wave his hand, there is a little boy in my class in Bnei Brak and his name is Shvartze Wolf and he's named after his *alter, alter zeide* Shvartze Wolf who told the story to the Belzer Rebbe.

I'm begging you, my friends. Please, keep on telling the story. Keep remembering Shvartze Wolf.

Do you know how many *Shvartze Wolfs* are walking around Yerushalayim? Yerushalayim is filled with *tzaddikim*.

If you see some obnoxious people, you never know. You really never know.

❧

Yerushalayim comes from the words, *"Yarei shalem"* — complete awe.

Is there any place in the world where the Ribbono Shel Olam reveals His love for us more than Yerushalayim?

Is there any city in the world which people love more?

French people love Paris, but not the way we love Yerushalayim.

Americans don't love Washington the way we love Yerushalayim.

What is the secret of Yerushalayim? Why do we love it so much?

Imagine that I love my wife very much and I bring her a gift. First, I say to her, "I brought you an unbelievable gift," and then I show it to her.

That is how it works. First, I tell her it is a gift and then I show it to her.

I don't first show her the gift and then say, "By the way, it's a gift."

The Ribbono Shel Olam says to Avraham Avinu, "Go to the land which I will show you," and only later does He say, "I will also give it to you and to your children."

It doesn't make sense.

First, He showed him the land, and only then He said it was a gift?

The Ribbono Shel Olam should have said to Avraham Avinu, "I'm going to give you the Holy Land, now I'll take you there and show you what the gift is."

What's going on here?

There is one place in the world that I love so much. For me, it's the most special place — the only place where my heart is fully open. This place touches the deepest secrets of my heart. Every person has this one place.

Now, let's go back to my wife.

In this case, with my most favorite place, first I'm going to tell her, "I want to show you that place which is most, most special to me," and then I say, "You know something, I'm giving it to you as a gift."

Because I love her so much, and because I love the place so much, I want to make sure she understands what the gift is. So she has to see it first in order to appreciate what I'm giving to her. She'll see how special *it* is to me, and then she'll know how special *she* is to me. In this case, she needs to see it first.

When it comes to giving a birthday present to your boss who you don't like, a gift that isn't really necessarily coming from the heart, you don't need to see it first. Tell the person it's a gift. For gifts like this, the idea of the gift is more special than the gift itself. First tell them you're giving a gift, then let them see it.

But when you are giving your heart, your soul, your most special place in the world — you want the person to see it first. To understand what you are giving.

Reb Leibe'le Eiger asks, why is it that until Avraham Avinu came, there was no Holy Land? He explains that until Avraham Avinu came, there was nobody in the world who was close enough to G-d that G-d should reveal to them His most favorite place — because Eretz Yisrael is the Ribbono Shel Olam's favorite place.

If I should have the privilege, if one of my daughters would take me to a place and tell me this is my favorite place, do you know suddenly that place looks different for me? It could be a tree and a little grass but now, after they tell me that this is their favorite place, it's not a tree anymore, it's not grass anymore; it's something else....

That little tree and little piece of grass is not special to me because *I* love it. It's special to me because *you* love it so much. That is the deepest *yirah* in the world.

I love Yerushalayim because it's G-d's favorite place. This is why every Yid comes to Yerushalayim. Sure, it's also our most favorite place, but it is only our most favorite place because it's the Ribbono Shel Olam's favorite place.

He loved it first.

Let's say I love someone. I show them my favorite place. Then they say that this place looks stupid.

Do you know what that means? It means that they are not connected to my soul. If my children would open up and show me their most favorite place and I say, "This place is meaningless," it means I have no *yirah* before my children.

When someone shows me their favorite place, I'm not looking with my eyes. I'm looking with their eyes. I'm looking with G-d's Eyes.

When someone you love loves a place, you love that place too.

G-d loves Yerushalayim, so I do too.

When someone gives me a present, why should I share it with anybody else?

Why should I say: *"Ki beisi beis tefillah yikare l'chol ha'amim"*?[51]

Why should I invite all the nations of the world to come to Yerushalayim? It's crazy, G-d gave me a present, a little land — I'm keeping it for myself!

You know what I want to share with the world? I want to show them G-d's most favorite place. It's true, G-d gave it to me. Still, I want to say to the world, "If you could only see G-d's favorite place — then, your hearts will open. Only then will you stand before G-d and pray for the first time."

The sin of the Tree of Knowledge was looking at everything with your own eyes, your own judgment: "This is right, this is wrong."

---

51 Yishayahu 56:7

It gets even worse. Everybody knows that crying comes from the eyes. Not only did we look at Yerushalayim with the wrong eyes — we cried over what our eyes initially saw. Not only do you look at G-d's favorite place with your own silly eyes — but you even cry over what looks to you like a difficult place?

At the time of the spies, we didn't get Eretz Yisrael because we didn't look at it with G-d's Eyes.

Later, we were driven out of Eretz Yisrael because we didn't know how to look at another Yid with G-d's Eyes.

The *tikun* (fixing) happens when I'm looking at everything with G-d's Eyes. His Eyes are different eyes; completely different eyes.

Suddenly it is so clear to me that every Yid is so holy, that Eretz Yisrael is so holy.

Why is Eretz Yisrael so holy? Because it's G-d's favorite place.

Why is Yerushalayim so holy? *"V'zeh shaar shamayim"* — "This is the door to G-d's House."[52] That is holy!

Ya'akov Avinu never said, "I like this place, it looks beautiful — let me call a photographer. I'd love a photo of this."

He said *"Ein ze ki im beis Elokim v'zeh shaar shamayim."*

Yerushalayim is the gate to G-d.

We have to look at another Jew with G-d's Eyes.

We have to look at Eretz Yisrael with G-d's Eyes.

We have to look at Yerushalayim with G-d's Eyes.

But it's not enough. Not enough.

"Dabru al lev Yerushalayim," — "Speak to the heart of Jerusalem."[53]

The heart is the deepest thing there is. It is deeper than my eyes. It is the deepest depths there is. We can't just use our eyes. Even G-d's Eyes are not enough. We need to use our hearts. Only our hearts can really feel His heart. Only our hearts can really feel Yerushalayim.

---

52 Bereishis 28:17
53 Yishayahu 40:2

How do you know when you love somebody very much? At that moment, there is no world. There is nothing else. Your brain, your eyes — they don't matter. All that matters is your heart.

What does it mean to remember somebody? I walk up to somebody I like very much and I tell them, "I remember you."

What does it mean? I also remember that Richard Nixon was President of the United States. Is this the same level?

There are different levels. I can remember a fact, but it doesn't matter to me. That is one level.

Another level, higher, is that when I remember you, everything else is forgotten. Nothing else matters.

What does it mean when I say that I always remember Yerushalayim? It means that when I say the word "Yerushalayim,"' nothing else exists. This is a much higher level. This is a holy level.

There is even a deeper level — when everything in the world reminds me of you. There's so much connected that everything in the world reminds me of you. It's my memory of you. Everything in the world is connected to my memory. This is the deepest level. In this way, I am *always* remembering Yerushalayim because everything reminds me of it. It means that I can walk in Amsterdam and look up to the sky and I don't know where I am — because it reminds me of Yerushalayim.

Everything reminds me of Yerushalayim. I never forget the Holy City. My heart is always in the Holy City, and nothing else matters. The Holy City is mine. It belongs to me, wherever I am.

Yerushalayim is in my heart. It *is* my heart.

Do you know how good it feels when you meet somebody who is familiar?

You walk down the streets in Paris, you don't know anyone, basically you love Paris, it's a beautiful city, but suddenly you meet somebody from your hometown. And you're so happy.

Let me ask something stupid: If you were so happy at home, why are you in Paris?

I took a vacation because I have to get out of town, but I'm so happy to meet someone who is familiar.

On one hand, I like to make my borders wider. I like to go to a place which I have never been to before.

On the other hand, in a crazy way, I would love so much to connect with something familiar. I miss home.

I want the old, and I want the new.

Imagine I travel to Hong Kong, I go to Japan, going to Australia, and I stay in the fanciest hotels, then I come home to my little house.

Why am I suddenly so happy? Let's face it, the Sheraton in Hong Kong is more beautiful than my little house.

But it doesn't matter.

I like the new, but this new doesn't belong to me yet, I'm just looking around.

The Ishbitzer says:

Do you know what it means when something is familiar — spiritually? What does it mean that something belongs to you?

On the one hand, I want something new — something which doesn't belong to me. On the other hand, I want something old, which *does* belong to me.

We need both. We need the new and we need the old.

Think about it: Why do so many marriages break up?

Husband and wife belong to each other, but it's getting on my nerves. It is old. I want something which doesn't belong to me. I want something else. But that won't make me happy — because we belong to each other, we need each other.

Same thing with Torah.

On one hand, young people want to be Jewish, Yiddishkeit is theirs, but it is old. It needs to be new. We need to make it fresh. But it also needs to be old. Yerushalayim feels so new, but it is so old.

What is the secret of Yerushalayim?

Yerushalayim belongs to me. It is my home. I come back to it.

❧

When you stand up to pray, you have to connect yourself to something. Believe it or not, it's not enough to connect yourself to G-d.

That's very holy but you have to be connected to the Holy Land as well. You have to stand facing Yerushalayim, the Holy Temple, and the Holy of Holies.

Let's say I'm in Acapulco and suddenly I remember that I've got to daven Minchah. I'm pretty far away from Yerushalayim.

Now imagine that not only I am far away physically, but I'm far away spiritually as well: I've completely forgotton that I am a Jew.

Out of nowhere, I'm reminded. Maybe I overheard words from heaven. How can I connect myself within seconds?

Today, you can call up a friend in Melbourne in a minute.

Spiritual dialing goes even faster.

When I start to daven, I connect myself to the Holy of Holies, and all it takes is to face the Holy of Holies.

Face Yerushalayim and you connect to Yerushalayim.

Why?

Do you think G-d cares if you stood with your back toward Yerushalayim? If I'm standing in Hawaii and my face is toward Yerushalayim, who cares? You can't see Yerushalayim from here; there's so many oceans, so much land, so many people in between.

The whole thing is ridiculous! When you stand toward the east, you're okay but when you stand toward the west, it's bad?

Why does it matter?

It *does* matter.

The physical, the spiritual, the divine, it's all one. Physically standing toward Yerushalayim is the greatest, holiest thing in the world.

I want you to know a true story:

There was a big war between the Turks and the Austrians in the seventeenth century. The land went back and forth; the Turks took it, the Austrians took it, the Turks took it back.

And there was one mountain, a very, very important mountain in the war in the area of Yugoslavia. Suddenly, while the fighting was very hard, this top general of the Austrians sees a little *Yiddele* from the Turkish side crossing the lines and walking up the mountain.

The *Yiddele* had a little Tehillim in his hands and a *tallis*. The general can't believe it. In the middle of this fighting? It is so dangerous! Also, maybe he's a spy?

So the general goes to him and asks, "Are you crazy? Who are you?"

The *Yiddele* says, "On top of this mountain there is a place that when you stand there, you can see Yerushalayim."

The general says, "I don't believe it, I don't believe it," but he was somehow taken by this *Yiddele*. Strange, here in Yugoslavia there's a mountain you can see Yerushalayim? It's not even such a way up, very high mountain; it must have been a very, very special high mountain. Who knows what kind of a mitzvah a *Yiddele* did there that from there you could see Yerushalayim.

The general says, "According to law I have to kill you because you might be a spy or something. But I'll tell you what. If you let me see Yerushalayim also, I'll let you go."

This *Yiddele* walked up there and he was sitting there on top of the mountain. Can you imagine what he saw and the way he saw it?

And this little non-Jewish general sitting next to him forgot the war — forgot the whole world.

They *mamesh* saw Yerushalayim.

After that, this general became a great friend of the Jews.

Now listen to this.

You can see Yerushalayim from anywhere, if you know how.

There is a very simple way of seeing Yerushalayim when you are in Hawaii. You just stand there facing Yerushalayim and you begin to daven. If you want to — you can see it.

If you can't see it, it means you weren't really interested. When you fly, they sell you those earphones to show you movies and they tell you it costs $2.50. If you really want to see the movie, you pay. If you don't pay, you're really not that interested in seeing the movie.

When you begin to daven, Eliyahu HaNavi comes — and says "Brother, I have some earphones for you. They cost very little. Just a little concentration, a little joy, a little cleaning of your *kishkes* — of your heart. Then you get the earphones and the special glasses. It is worth it. I'll show you something strong."

Some of us say, "I'm sophisticated. I don't believe in all this nonsense."

But if you really want to hear, if you really want to see, you'll get the earphones or special glasses from Eliyahu HaNavi. Then you'll really hear. Then you'll really see.

It's true. You can connect yourself to the Holy of Holies. The High Priest only walked into it once a year on Yom Kippur. Today is just a regular day. It's Wednesday, but it doesn't matter. When you pack yourself G-d's earphones or holy glasses, you can see everything, absolutely everything.

Everybody knows that Reb Hershele Riminover could see from one corner of the world to the other. So he met this *misnaged* who said,"Rebbe, I can't understand you. Don't you believe what the Gemara says that prophecy was taken away after the destruction of the Temple and given only to children and to fools?"

So Reb Hershele says "That's prophecy? To see from one corner of the world to the other? Do you think G-d gave me eyes only to see what's in front of me? When G-d gave me eyes, he gave me eyes to see everything. Prophecy is something even deeper than that which you don't even know of."

We think G-d gave us eyes just to see the glass of coffee on the table. It is very beautiful, but G-d gave me eyes for something deeper than that.

He gave me eyes to see beyond.

And my heart sees even further.

If I open my heart, my heart of hearts, I can always — no matter where I am — see Yerushalayim.

※

There are two kinds of relationships.

There's a relationship on the level of learning. It is a relationship of the mind. It is holy, very holy. Still, it is finite. When I'm learning, I don't have to face Yerushalayim. I don't have to be connected to Yerushalayim.

There's a different kind of relationship between people. It is on the level of prayer. On the level of praying — you face Yerushalayim.

Learning is very high. I'm making myself a vessel so that holy wisdom should flow into me.

Praying is different. Praying means that I open my soul which is infinite.

I open my heart, my soul, my life before G-d — and before my close, close friend.

You can always tell what kind of relationship people have. When I see a husband and wife talk loudly to each other, forget it. Their relationship may be okay. It may be functional. It may be intellectual, but it is not on the level of prayer.

When they always talk softly to each other, that is different. The husband says to the wife, "What time is it?" and she says "It's nine o'clock" real softly — these few words on the level of prayer. This little house is a real Beis Hamikdash. When you're there, you can see the Holy of Holies.

What kind of relationship do you have to the people you love? A relationship of the mind or of the heart? Of learning or of prayer? The deeper you love, the more it has to be a prayer. The heart. The soul.

What kind of relationship do you have with Yerushalayim? With Yerushalayim, it can only be a relationship of prayer. Of the heart. Of the soul.

To be a "Yerushalayim Yid," you need to learn to pray.

We have to teach our children how to learn. They don't know how to on their own.

We don't have to teach our children how to pray because they know how. What is the first thing a baby does when it is born? Crying. The first thing a baby does in the whole world is praying. A baby, when it's a little bit hungry it begins to cry. It's body is crying for food. But it's soul is turning to the Beis Hamikdash because the little baby doesn't know anything else.

The same is true for us. We think that we need to learn how to pray but it isn't true.

We don't have to learn how to pray or what to pray. All we have to do is unlearn, and get back to our real selves.

Our hearts pray. Our souls pray. They do it naturally. And they pray toward Yerushalayim, the center of everything.

Reb Nachman says that there are two kinds of hearts.

There is the *lev hatachton* and *lev haelyon* — a lower heart and a higher heart.[54]

Imagine that I'm invited to my best friend's daughter's wedding. I really love my friend and his daughter is very special to me as well. I'm very much touched and I'm dancing like mad, but it's still my lower heart.

But when I'm at *my* daughter's wedding, that's my high heart, and this heart reaches somewhere else, somewhere so deep inside.

Have you heard people say that if you are a real holy man, you have to love all the children of the world like you love your own?

---

54 *Likutei Moharan* 1:20

That's stupid. This is not the way G-d created the world. G-d created the world that I know something about my children, which nobody knows. G-d wants me to love my children more than somebody else. Of course, you've got to love the whole world, but not like your own kids.

With your own kids, it is the *lev elyon*. It is so much deeper.

And here I want you to open your hearts in the deepest depths.

You can learn the Torah with your lower heart. But the real explanation of the Torah, the deepest meaning of it, comes from the *lev haelyon*.

The *lev haelyon* is so complete and so holy. When something touches my high heart, I realize it was always there to begin with. It is not new at all.

How do I know that I met my soul mate? At a certain point, when I look at my soul mate, I know that I've known her for 2,000 years. In fact, I can't even imagine that there was a time I didn't know her. It was always written on my heart.

When I see somebody else's child, it's beautiful. It's the first time I see this baby. It is nice and cute, but it is new. Completely new.

My own child? Was there ever a time I didn't know my children? Could I ever stand before G-d and not know my children? It's impossible.

The low heart is good. But the real action — that is the high heart. That's what it's all about.

It says in the Torah, "*L'ovdo b'chol l'vavchem*," you need to serve G-d with your hearts.[55] You have to serve G-d with your lower heart, and you have to serve G-d with your high heart. When it comes to learning Torah, and even keeping different parts of the Torah, maybe you can make it with your low heart. Maybe. But some things need more.

When it comes to praying, you need your high heart. Praying is *avodah shebalev*, the service of the heart. You need the entire thing, lower and higher. Otherwise, it is just words. Do you really think this is what G-d desires?

---

55 Devarim 11:13

Another example: You can keep every Shabbos to the letter of the law for 2 million years, but unless Shabbos reaches the high heart, the deepest, highest place in your heart, you didn't feel it yet. You haven't really kept Shabbos yet. It was all just superficial. It didn't touch your *kishkes*. That's not the kind of Shabbos G-d wants for us, friends.

It needs to be real.

You need the higher heart.

But what is it? What is the higher heart?

The *lev haelyon*, the high heart, is when I look into the Torah and it becomes written on my heart. "*Kasvem al luach libecha*," — "Inscribe the words on the tablets of your heart."[56]

How do you know when it is *mamesh* inscribed in your heart? When I realize I can't do without it. I could never do without it. I simply can't be without it.

What's so special about the heart? G-d forbid, a person can live without their feet, or their ears. Sad, very sad — but you can do it.

You can't live without your heart. When the Torah reaches these depths of me, when it reaches the heart — you just can't be without it.

If I learn something and I don't understand it, I'll turn to the next page.

If you do that, you'll never understand it.

When you see the words and you don't understand them, how fast are you praying to begin to understand? How fast do you cry out to G-d, begging Him to open your heart to not just understand the words you are learning, but to *feel* the words as well?

When I know this, when I pray this, then G-d reveals to me the deepest depths of the Torah and the way it's revealed to me that I *mamesh* see it is written on my heart. It was written on my heart all the time. I *did* understand it. I understood it all the time.

We pray for a lot of things. A lot of very important things, holy things.

---

56   Mishlei 7:2

What is the deepest prayer in the world? What does the highest heart pray for?

The deepest prayer is not that I should have all I need. That is very deep.

The deepest prayer in the world is, "Can you please, G-d, explain to me my life. Can I have just a little explanation of what is happening?"

When I am learning, the deepest depth is not that I want to understand what it says. That is very important, and is a very holy thing.

But the deepest depth is that I want to know, "How does it relate to me?"

Now listen to this.

The deepest depth of Shabbos is not that I don't drive a car on Shabbos, that I do everything. I want G-d to reveal to me why it is that I can never be without this one Shabbos And this is the deepest explanation there is. G-d reveals that to me this absolute deepest, deepest depths. But now I want you to go one step further.

Why, G-d, did You put me in this world? Why now?

Why here?

I would love to know what am I doing in this space, what am I doing in this life. What do You need me for?

Imagine that I am very friendly with somebody else, but they absolutely don't need me in their lives. They have everything they need. They don't need me. It's cute and sweet. When they see me, they smile.

But when they don't see me, they are also smiling. They can do without me.

Do you know what goes wrong with parents and children? When, suddenly, children realize that parents are not the center of their lives. They can get along without their parents. Do you know what the saddest thing is for parents? When they realize suddenly that they are not in the center of their children's lives.

The heart is the center. The center of the world.

It would be a great honor to be connected to G-d's foot, so to speak. A great honor to be connected to G-d's ear, humanly speaking.

But we can do more. We can connect to G-d's Heart. Yerushalayim is G-d's Heart.

A body needs its heart. The world needs its heart.

So now, let's see where Reb Nachman takes this to.

Reb Nachman says that Mount Sinai is the headquarters for *lev hatachton*, the low heart.

But *Yerushalayim Ir HaKodesh*, Yerushalayim the Holy City, is the headquarters for the higher heart.

So therefore it says "*Ki mitziyon teytzeh Torah u'dvar Hashem M'Yerushalayim*." "For from Zion, Torah will come out, and the word of G-d from Yerushalayim."[57] Have you ever thought about that verse?

Everybody knows that the Torah was given on Mount Sinai! Suddenly, it says "*Ki mitziyon teytzeh Torah u'dvar Hashem M'Yerushalayim*"?

So this is what Reb Nachman says. The Torah itself was given on Mount Sinai, but the explanation of the Torah, its deepest depths are written on my high heart. This is a completely different level. After I learn it, it is written on my heart — this is only in Yerushalayim.

Yerushalayim is not just buildings. It is not even just the Holy Wall. It is so much more. It is the gate for the Holy Land in it's entirety.

How do you merit to have a part in the Holy Land? Only when you reach the level of *lev haelyon*.

If I only have a low heart, I can make it in Brooklyn, I can make it in Alaska. I can even fulfill every word of the Torah.

But to be part of the Holy Land, you must have a *lev haelyon*.

Obviously, when people come to Yerushalayim, to the Holy City; do you think they just want to know where G-d is? They want to know where *they* are. It's not that they don't know where they are. They *mamesh* want G-d to reveal to them: What am I doing in this world right now. And, also, please G-d can You tell me; why can't You do it without me?

Now I want you to know the deepest depths.

Imagine somebody calls me up in the middle of the night, at four

---

57   Yishayahu 2:3

o'clock and says "I have a party, I know you're asleep but I have an absolutely beautiful party at my place, could you please come over." I say "Really, thank you for inviting me, but I'm really tired."

There is one thing which would make me come to the party: If the person says to me, "I have a party but we absolutely can't do without you," I'm jumping up and I'm going. The moment I know they can't do without me — nothing is hard. Nothing is hard. You know why everything comes on so hard? Because we always think the world can do without us.

Any place I have to go to is already basically a sign it's not my home. To my own house, I don't *have* to go. So why do I go? Because my house can't be without me. It's my house. It's where my heart is. *Mamesh*. My highest heart. My house needs me. Yerushalayim needs me.

※

There is a Tree of Life and there is a Land of Life. The Tree of Life is only a tree. The Land of Life is something else.

Eretz Yisrael is called *Eretz Hachayim*, the Land of Life.

How do you know that something is alive? What is a sign of life?

A sign of life is to grow and to expand.

Do you know when Israel became the Land of Life? When it was given to Ya'akov.

Ya'akov Avinu passed by Yerushalayim when he was fleeing from Esav. He went over the border and was already outside of Israel. As soon as left the Holy Land, he said to himself "How could I pass by Yerushalayim without praying?"

The sun went down. He prayed and then fell asleep. The Gemara says that at that exact moment, Yerushalayim came to Ya'akov.[58] The Beis Hamikdash came to Ya'akov.

Can you imagine how Yerushalayim expanded?

---

58 Tractate *Chulin* 91b

Avraham and Yitzchak were on the level that the Holy Land was given to them.

Ya'akov was something else. Wherever Ya'akov is, this is where the Holy Land is. Ya'akov can take Yerushalayim in his hands and bring it outside of Eretz Yisrael.

This is the difference between the Land and the Tree. The Tree of Life is very beautiful, but it's in one place. The Land of Life can reach the whole world.

The Medrash says "*Asida Eretz Yisrael shetispashet b'chol ha'aratzos*," "Someday Israel will expand all over the world."[59] Not the Tree of Knowledge and not the Tree of Life, but the Land of Life. The whole world will be as holy as Israel, and this is the level of Ya'akov Avinu.

It is alive. It grows. It is the heart.

According to our tradition, on Shabbos you have to be in a different place than the rest of the week. You have to be higher.

Everybody knows that G-d created Adam and Eve on Friday, the sixth day of Creation. According to our tradition, on that very day they ate the forbidden fruit and just one second before sunset they were driven out from Paradise. They just missed it.

On Shabbos, the whole world has the chance to go back to Paradise. We can do the fixing.

But go back to the Garden of Eden. Imagine if Adam and Eve would not have been driven out from Paradise. Where would they go for Shabbos? They had to be somewhere higher than wherever they currently were.

The answer is that G-d would have taken them to Yerushalayim. Yerushalayim is even higher than Paradise! Why? Paradise — heaven, has a little opposite: Hell. So it is good, really good, but there is something connected to it, opposite it, that is bad. That is high. But it isn't *glatt*. It isn't the Highest.

There has to be something so holy that it has no opposite, there is nothing low or bad connected to it in any way. This is the Yerushalay-

---

59 *Yalkut Shimoni Yishayahu*, Taf Kuf Gimel (503)

im which we haven't tasted yet. The Yerushalayim that we know now is the Yerushalayim which is below Paradise.

The Yerushalayim which is above Paradise — *Yerushalayim shel ma'alah* — hasn't been revealed to us yet.

This is what the world is getting more and more ready for, for this new Yerushalayim. For the heart, the *lev elyon*. For *Yerushalayim shel ma'alah*.

❧

Imagine I walk on the street and I see a poor man and all I have on me is a dollar. So I'm thinking to myself, *Should I give him just half a dollar and leave half a dollar for myself or should I give him all I have?*

Let's say that something happens and I feel very high and I give him all I have. That comes from the "all of me." My "all of me" gives "all" to the poor man, but it's not really "all" there is. No person has more than "all they have." But imagine if there would be such a thing that not only the "all of me," but the "all" of my world. If I would be the Master of the World and I am giving you not only the "all" of me, but the whole world, even I can do it because I can; but there is such a thing, *mamesh*, "all there is."

And here I want you to open your hearts till the end of the world. There are certain things which affect my soul in the deepest way once I'm already in this world, and there are certain things which touch the essence of my being which are part of me even before I came into this world.

I can connect to a person on two levels, I can love a person on two levels. I'm already in this world and I know you so I love you. But then there is something much deeper. Sometimes I can love a person so much that it touches my very being in this world.

Imagine a Chinese man, he is connected to Peking and a *Yiddele* is connected to Yerushalayim. I'm sure that "all" of the Chinese man is connected to Peking, but this is the kind of the "all'" which is after I am created. After he is already created as a Chinese man, then he is connected to Peking. If he cannot be in Peking so he lives in New York; he forgets about Peking. Who he is is much more important than where he is. For a *Yiddele*, Yerushalayim is not connected after my creation. It touches the very foundation of my creation. If not Yerushalayim, I can't have something else, cannot exchange it.

The more outside something is the more the little bit is also meaningful. Imagine I'll make a deal with Coca Cola. I would like to sell you 10,000 bottles of Coca Cola. My friend tells me, "Well, my soul is not that big, I cannot use 10,000 bottles but I would be glad to buy 1,000 from you."

For anything that comes from the outside, a little bit is also good. Imagine that I am very hungry and I walk into this restaurant and I ask for five steaks and ten hamburgers and they tell me "Listen, brother, we are just closing up. All I can give you is a leftover donut." Since I am so hungry, I will take it because it's outside of me. Now listen to this, on a physical level: The more outside it is, the less complete it has to be. It should be complete but if it's not it is possible, okay.

G-d forbid, we should have all our feet, but if one foot is missing, I can still live. If someone might say "I'm going to cut off half of my heart G-d forbid, so I'm living on half," it just doesn't go because the heart is the inside of my inside and the inside of my inside has to be complete.

Let me tell you something. Imagine I am giving a speech on Maoism and I'm speaking to the Chinese and they don't understand exactly what I say, because maybe I am speaking in Hebrew. In the meantime I am telling them that it doesn't matter, they understood a little bit, it served its purpose.

But imagine that I want to propose to the woman I love and I say three words to her, "I love you." And she says "I didn't hear the two last words." It just doesn't go. When it comes to the deepest depths of life, when it comes to the real things, unless it's complete, it's not there.

So you see, until our home in Yerushalayim is completely there — we are not complete.

6
The Holiness of Connection

How do you know if you love somebody? It's very simple. How close do you feel to them when you think of them? I'm thinking now that next week I have to meet a producer and he is going to talk to me about a concert. I'll meet him, we'll talk, and that will be it. When I'm thinking of him, I don't feel any different.

Do you know what happened to me yesterday? I was thinking to myself, *Today I'll see my child again*. And in that one second, my soul was already *mamesh* together with my child. Something else.

Imagine that you want to say something bad about another person and it's just bugging you so much and you just can't control yourself. But imagine if you would make up your mind that each time you want to say something bad about another person, before you do it, you think of Yerushalayim. You won't be able to do it because Yerushalayim is so holy; the vibrations are so strong. After thinking of Yerushalayim, you can't say anything bad about anyone.

Do you know what it means to always remember Yerushalayim? It's not just "don't forget it." When you think of it, something happens to you. You feel different. You are different. Something happens to you. Some people, some places, some ideas — they change you.

Imagine, I am interested in becoming a Jew, and I go to this great Rabbi who teaches me all about Yiddishkeit. Suddenly, he gave me life. But after I learned everything, I broke away from it. I said that I don't really need it all — it's too complicated. It doesn't help anyway. I forgot the whole thing.

Many years later, I meet this Rabbi on the street and he says to me, "Hey Shloimele, how are you?" And I tell him, "I changed, I'm on a different trip now." He goes home and I go home.

But, maybe, just maybe, I realize that I've got to go back to him. All his teaching was on the level of not only giving me life — but bringing me back to life.

That's what Yerushalayim is. Yerushalayim always brings you back.

I heard a very sweet Torah from an old Slonimer chassid. He said there are two kinds of medications. There are prescriptions, and then there is another kind of medicine. If *chas v'shalom* you are in the hospital, and the patients are up late at night because they can't sleep, what do they do? They walk around telling each other "I took this medicine, and I took this medicine." When this happens, you learn about medicine not on a doctor level, but on a friend level.

I want to share something very deep with you.

We always think that, physically, we need a good doctor. This medication, aspirin, Excedrin... they only help sometimes. But the Ishbitzer says its the other way around. For spiritual prescriptions, you go to a Rebbe. But when Mashiach is coming, it will be like "*Kol tzofayich kol nasu yachadav*" — "The voice of your lookouts, together they raise their voice."[60]

Yidden will tell each other, "I don't need a doctor, I *mamesh* need a good friend to fix me." The other Yid will say "I'm sick and tired of all the doctors, I need one good friend, can you please, maybe help me?"

Those two Yidden will be the ushers for Mashiach to come.

---

60   Yishayahu 52:8

You know what all of Israel needs?

We don't need a doctor, we need connection. We each need one good friend.

༄

I want to share one of the deepest concepts in the *Zohar*. It's one of the foundations of Jewish mysticism. At first, it might sound simple — but it really isn't.

In Hebrew, whenever you want to say the word "and," you always use the letter *vav*.[61] The *Zohar* teaches: "*Kodesh*" (holy) can be written with a *vav* or without a *vav*. The letter *vav* is the letter of connection.

That means that there are two types of holiness in the world. There is a holiness which is without a *vav*, without a connection, and there is holiness with a connection.

The *Zohar HaKadosh* says that the holiness we see and know in this world is holiness of connection: it is within the framework of the world.

What's a holy person in this world? A person who is connected to holiness. A person who does everything holy is a holy person. Sometimes you meet a thief, a drunkard, an underground person who is the lowest, but you sense something so beautiful in this person. It's not connected to his light in the least. This person has something from G-d inside. He is connected. That is the holiness with the *vav* — it is connected to something outside of itself. It is holy, very holy.

The *Zohar* explains, though, that the holiness of G-d has no *vav*. G-d's holiness is deeper than connection.

Sometimes you can be in love with somebody very much and everything connects, but what's missing? That holiness which is deeper than connection. I have seen Rabbis where everything is Jewish and yet when it comes to a certain point, something is missing. They don't have this holiness beyond connection.

---

61 *Zohar* 3 94b

Pouring out my heart is not connection, it's deeper than connection. If I am connected to you on the level which is beyond connection, if I am connected to G-d on the level of *kodesh* without the *vav*, then I can pour out my heart. I can walk on the street and meet a stranger and pour out my heart and soul before him; I don't know his name and he doesn't know mine... we have this holiness beyond connection.

What's happening in the world? There is suddenly an unbelievable awakening, there is such a deep awakening where people want to know the secrets of life. The first awakening is not that I am looking for the holiness of connection. I don't want someone telling me to do this and don't do that. It doesn't have to connect to the way I eat my ice cream. I am waiting for someone to give me this holiness which is deeper than connection. I want to experience something so deep. Hopefully, that holiness will lead me to find the holiness of connection.

We need the holiness of connection, but we also need the holiness beyond connection.

Do you know what it is to be in exile? To be in exile means that I'm disconnected from this holiness which is beyond connection. While you're in exile, a slave can also be holy. I can do everything I want to, why not? A slave can be holy, a slave can be honest.

What does it mean to be in exile? Exile means that I am disconnected from that holiness which is deeper than connection. Something inside doesn't feel right, the deepest inside doesn't reach me.

I want you to know something unbelievably deep. Do you know how the world wants to bring peace? The world wants to bring peace between nations on the level of the holiness of connection, one nation should connect to the other.

Let's face it, on the level of connection we are disconnected. Unfortunately, they start at the wrong end. It has to start from those depths which are deeper than connection, much deeper than connection.

And here I want you to open your hearts. The Holy Temple is a place where you get your holiness which is deeper than connection. Only in the Beis Hamikdash.

Moshe and Aharon are the two masters of the Jewish People. Moshe is the master of Mount Sinai and Aharon is the master of the Holy Temple. Mount Sinai is about connection. On Mount Sinai, G-d tells you what to do and what not to do, what to believe in and what not to believe in. It is absolutely necessary, absolutely holy, and absolutely the holiness of connection.

In the Holy Temple, nobody gives you a speech, you just come there and you pray and pour out your heart. You'll connect later when you walk away, but there is something much deeper than connection. This is where Aharon HaKohen shines brighter than ever.

When G-d spoke to Moshe by the burning bush, Moshe argued with G-d for a whole week because he wanted his brother, Aharon, to receive the Ten Commandments on Mount Sinai, and he wanted Aharon to redeem the Jews from Egypt. Why? It wasn't just humility, although it was also that. On a deeper level, Moshe Rabbeinu wanted the Jews to first receive this holiness beyond connection. Obviously, we weren't ready yet.

We always have trouble with Yerushalayim. On Mount Sinai, nobody stops us, we have all the books. On the level of connection, this is not our problem. The problem is Yerushalayim, the Holy City, the city of this awesome holiness.

Some people judge prayers according to how long they last.

If you pray for one hour that's pretty good.

If you pray for half an hour, who knows? If you pray for just one minute, then for sure it's nothing — you think G-d bothers to listen for a minute?

In Kotsk, maybe they spent ten hours on preparation, but the most important thing was not how long the prayers were — but how much did you pour out your heart? In the synagogue, we are missing the outpouring of the heart.

When I pray, I ask G-d to give me this and give me that. It's all connection. When I pour out my heart before G-d, it is deeper than connection. I'm not even asking anything — I'm just pouring out my heart.

Let's says that ten years ago I had a very close friend. *Mamesh* the closest. Then we lose track of each other. I meet him ten years later in Paris. I walk down the street and he says, "Oh, hi, how are you?" Wonderful, ordinary talk, "See ya, *zie gezunt*."

Ten years ago, it was alive. Then it died.

Now imagine that you are very close to someone and you meet them fifty years later, and all the feelings in the world come right back to you.

There are some people that you are so close to that whenever you see them, you are in the middle of a sentence. You just continue on from the last time you talked. They are the people that bring you back. You are different when you are with them, and you never forget them. They bring you back. You can't wait to be with them again.

This is what Yerushalayim is all about.

To the first person, it was the level of connection. On the level of connection it's repetition; you are connected or you're not.

If I am connected to somebody on the level which is deeper than connection then I can say "I love you" 100 times. It's still not enough because it's *mamesh* infinite. It's G-d's level, its G-d's holiness. That holiness which is so deep....

Do you know what this level of beyond connection does? In a way, it connects us to everything which is truly meaningful and important in our lives. Imagine I am going to the Holy City Yerushalayim, I am standing by the Holy Wall and I feel so Jewish and so holy, and suddenly I realize that everything in Yerushalayim connects to my life. It's beyond connection, but it's the ultimate connection.

It's the most beautiful and exalted feeling in the world.

We ran away *from* Egypt.

We are running *to* Yerushalayim.

This is important. Instead of running from something — run toward something.

It makes the whole difference.

When something hurts you, don't run away from your friends, this is the time to run to your friends.

Children, when they are little, what do they do, do they run away? No — they run *to* their parents.

When we get older, we get perverted, we run away from things.

Whenever a person is sad they want to run away from the world. They want to run away from themselves, and they want to run away from G-d. What happened to Adam and Eve? Their first mistake is that they ran away... away from G-d, from Paradise, and they began hiding.

Sometimes you talk to the person you love the most and you can't get through to them. They are hiding and building walls around themselves. They're running away, even though they're right there in front of you. What do you do?

Listen to this story. Reb Nosson, Reb Nachman's greatest pupil, had some kind of a distant cousin who was very wealthy. Suddenly, he went bankrupt and he ran away. He decided to go to Odessa where he had a rich uncle so he could take a loan from him. He passed by the city of Breslov, and by that time, after walking for a few weeks he was so downhearted and so broken. His shirt wasn't washed in months. He came to Reb Nosson and Reb Nosson says to him "Where are you going?" "I am going to a rich uncle in Odessa. I'll take a loan from him, a million rubles and I will reestablish my business." Reb Nosson says, "*Oy vey, gevalt* are you mistaken. The way you look like right now, he won't even let you into his house. He will put ten rubles in your hand and he will say that this is all he can do for you."

"So what should I do?" And this is what Reb Nosson told him: "Don't run away, go back to your city. Go back to your wife and to your children but even more, run to G-d. You are bankrupt and you have no business, go to the *beis medrash*. Go to the House of G-d, to the House of Prayer and learn day and night. You have no business no? Beautiful, it's time to learn and to pray. It's time to fill your heart with the holiest teachings in the world and Hashem will help you. Instead of running away, run to… run to the One, to the only One who can help."

He listened to Reb Nosson and went back to his city and the people didn't believe it. They knew he was bankrupt and that he ran away from all the people he owed so much money to. He's back, he's not running away? What is he doing? They were told that he is learning day and night.

People were so blown away that they gathered together a lot of money, gave him a loan and he reestablished his business.

When you run to G-d, leave it up to Him. When you run to your best friend, they will always help you.

If you are very, very sad, who can you run to? Who?

Instead of running away run to… run to the One, to the Only One.

You know what a true friend is? A true friend is someone who, when you tell them why you are sad, you are not sad anymore.

You know what the Holy Ba'al Shem Tov brought into the world? That everyone needs a Rebbe, a holy master. Every person in the world needs someone to go to, a good friend.

Every child needs a father and a mother, you know what a father and mother are for? Not to tell their children that they are doing wrong; that they know on their own. To have someone simply to run to, to run to.

When G-d says to Eve that she will have trouble having children after she ate from the Tree of Knowledge, she knew that she is in this world to raise children.

She thought to herself, *What is the greatest thing I can do for my children? I'll eat from the Tree of Knowledge and I will be able to tell them what is right and what is wrong.*

G-d says "Look at yourself, you are running away from me." You know what a mother is for? When her children are crying they will run to their mother. So G-d says "*Oy*, Chava'le, I am so sorry, I'm so sorry. It will be hard for you to have children but you don't know the secret what a mother is really for.... A mother is not only to teach right and wrong. A mother is to have someone to run to."

Let us stop running away from each other. Let's run together to the One, the only One.

Someday, the world will realize that there is no other way. Wars get us nowhere, hatred doesn't lead anywhere.

There is only one way: Let us all of us run to Yerushalayim, the Holy City. Let's run to the One, the only One. Let's connect to Him.

At that moment, the whole world will run to G-d and to each other, at that moment the world will be filled with joy. Do you know how beautiful it is to know that you have one good friend, that there is somebody who loves and wants to help me?

Now, sadly, it isn't always like this. We run away *from* things rather than running *to* them.

Don't disconnect. Always connect.

Always run *to*. Never run *away*.

☙

When you run *away* from things, you don't have a dream. You just want to get away from the pain, the sadness.

When you run *to* things, you need to know where and what you are running to. Where you want to go. Where you want to be. You need a dream.

The world is strange. You stop a little man and you will ask him "What do you eat bread for?" and he will answer "I need strength."

"What do you need strength for?" and he will tell you, "I have to fight because to live is to fight. Survival, making a few pennies, it's all about fighting."

The Hebrew language is so holy. The word for bread *lechem*, is the same letters as *lochem*, fighting.

The first man says he needs bread for fighting.

But then you will stop another little holy *Yiddele*, a little holy beggar, you will ask him "What do you eat bread for?" He will answer you, "I need strength to dream, I need strength to dream."

Strangely enough, *lechem* is also the same letters as *chalom*, dreaming. Some people eat to fight and some people eat to dream.

Dreaming when we sleep is beautiful. Everybody dreams when they are sleeping.

We need more. The people who rebuild Yerushalayim, are the people who dream when they are awake. To dream of a better world, to dream of a world which wakes up to realize that we all have the same dream. We are all crying for the same dream… we should eat — put bread in our mouths — to have the strength to dream of Yerushalayim.

We are trying to connect to Yerushalayim.

We are dreaming of Yerushalayim.

We are running to Yerushalayim.

7
Seeing with G-d's Eyes

I can walk in Yerushalayim and see a broken Wall.

But in the broken Wall, I can see the Beis Hamikdash.

We can meet people. Some people we meet are broken, but if we have really good eyes, you know how to look at them. You see the Beis Hamikdash in each and every one of them.

All we need is for someone to look at us with the right eyes. The spies came to Israel and they said it's a terrible country. The way it was, they were right, but why didn't they see how it would be in the future?

Didn't they know how it would look when Yidden will be there?

Imagine I go to the Holy Land, many years ago before we came back. A terrible country!

Imagine I have G-d's eyes. I would see how beautiful it is.

I could look at a person, and this person looks terrible!

If you have good eyes, you can see how beautiful they really are.

When there's sunlight, I don't need good eyes. Things are clear.

In the dark, then you need good eyes. When things aren't clear, that is when you need good eyes.

Imagine that I love my wife very much. On a street corner, we say goodbye. She goes her way, I go mine. After two minutes, I look around. We were looking at each other all the time. You know what that look is? It's so dark, it's so dark outside.

Where do I get what I need?

To *mamesh* make it in this world, I need Yerushalayim eyes. Those eyes that might have destruction right in front of them, but those same eyes see so much more than that.

~•~

Aharon HaKohen was the High Priest because he looked at every *Yiddele* while he was holding a candle. You know how beautiful people look in candlelight?

What's the difference between the sun, the moon, and a candle?

The Gemara says Moshe Rabbeinu is the sun. Yehoshua is the moon, and Aharon HaKohen is the Master of the candle.[62] With a candle, we see the deepest depths. Aharon brought peace, Aharon brought love and togetherness — because he had the eyes.

He had G-d's eyes, so he was able to bring us together. The more we get G-d's eyes, the more our lives come together. The more we see that we have what we need, we just never saw it before. We didn't have the right eyes.

~•~

What is the deepest thing in the world?

Life itself is the deepest thing in the world.

How do I connect to the depths of my life? Is it through what I see or what I hear?

Seeing is very high, but hearing is much deeper.

It doesn't take a deep person to see, but it takes a very, very deep person to hear.

So the Ishbitzer says like this. Seeing with your eyes is limited. You can only see the outside. You cannot see the inside.

---

62 Tractate *Bava Basra* 75a

When you listen, you get to the inside. Listening is the inside.

With your eyes, you can see destruction. You see the Inquisition, you see Auschwitz.

On the level of hearing, the greatest thing in the world is when you *mamesh* hear what the Ribbono Shel Olam is doing with us. If you have good ears, then you hear how G-d chooses us to be His People.

On the level of seeing, you see how He threw us out and how so many people still hate us and fight us.

On the level of hearing, I hear that He is taking us back.

In other words, on the level of seeing, it looks like G-d has forsaken you. On the level of hearing, you can see that G-d is concentrating just on you.

The Ishbitzer says something beautiful:[63]

When do I have trouble seeing the king? There are so many more subjects waiting to see him, until I want to see him I have to make an appointment and wait twenty years till I get to see him.

If I am the only person around, I have no trouble.

On the level of seeing, there are 2 billion people who want to see G-d.

On the level of hearing, it is just me and G-d, nobody else.

The way we translate the Hebrew word *shmi'a* is hearing, but the way the *Beis Ya'akov* translates *shmi'a* is not really hearing; *shmi'a* is these deepest depths of me which you understand.

When a person comes to me and says "Tell me something, where do you buy challahs for Shabbos?" —it has to do with hearing.

On the level of seeing, these words tell me "This person is looking for a bakery." But on the level of hearing, I hear that *gevalt*, he wants to be invited for Shabbos.

Sometime a *Yiddele* comes up to you and he says, "I don't believe in G-d anymore." On the level of seeing, this *Yiddele* is telling you he doesn't believe in G-d. On the level of hearing, he is saying "I so wish I felt close to G-d."

---

63 *Beis Yaakov* 52:8 Yishaya — Chodesh Menachem Av

Can you hear what the people you love are saying to you? Maybe they aren't using words, but they are speaking to you.

Can you hear it?

Can you hear what G-d is saying to you?

He is always speaking to each and every one of us.

Imagine someone who loves me very much writes me a letter. I put the letter somewhere and I can't find it. Do you know what I do? I turn over my whole house. I don't care if I break down the walls, I have got to find this letter. It's more important than the whole house.

If a person comes to me and sees that I am turning over the house, he says to me — on the level of seeing — "You are crazy, what are you doing to your house?"

If you are on the level of hearing, you understand that this is my house, I am not going to destroy it. I'm looking for something, something very, very important to me.

G-d is the same way. Can you imagine what kind of depths G-d is looking for us from that He is destroying the whole house just to find something? G-d is not really destroying anything. He wants to bring us to that deepest deepest depths, because if you have this deepest depths, the house can be rebuilt by itself. Who needs a house? What is a house without us? The Ribbono Shel Olam is looking for me in such a desperate way. Why did G-d destroy the Holy Temple? Simply because He is looking for me.

So now listen to this. Imagine you come into my house and you see my whole house upside down. You see me and my wife staring at our new baby. On the level of seeing, you don't see anything beautiful, you say "What's going on? This house looked so beautiful last time I was here. What's going on now? It's so dirty, everything is turned upside down."

On the level of hearing, all you notice is the parents looking at their baby. How beautiful! Everything is so beautiful.

On the level of seeing, the Holy Temple is destroyed. On the level of hearing, it says "*Hishlich Mishamayim Eretz*."[64] You can translate it in two ways. G-d threw down the beauty of Israel to the lowest depths. Or you can say that G-d threw heaven down to earth into Eretz Yisrael because Eretz Yisrael is so beautiful, Yidden are so beautiful. For them it's worth to throw heaven down to earth.

On the level of seeing, I'm just one Jew among other Jews.

On the level of hearing, it's just me and G-d.

༄

On the street, you need lights to see and lights to walk.

In my own house, I don't need light. I can walk around in the dark.

The house, the home, gives its own light. I hear the walls telling a story. I can't see it with my eyes, but what a light it gives!

The street is telling you things on the level of seeing. My house is on the level of hearing.

On a simple level, on a sweet level, I learned this from my baby. Once, I walked into the baby's room and the baby wasn't there. On the level of seeing, the baby wasn't there. On the level of hearing, *gevalt* did the walls tell me about my baby.

Towards the end, while His House was still standing, we didn't hear so well, so the Ribbono Shel Olam had no other way of making us hear.

When the Holy Temple was destroyed, though, everything changed. Do you know what happened?

We stopped hearing. The house didn't tell us anything anymore.

Today, it is so hard to hear.

The Beis Hamikdash, G-d's House, isn't speaking to us anymore.

It is very hard to hear.

We can hardly even see.

---

64 Eichah 2:1

On the other hand, the Temple *is* still speaking to us:

When I walk down the street, I see the house — I don't hear the house. You know when I hear the house? When someone destroys it, I can hear one stone rolling down from another stone.

So if G-d wants us not only to see the Holy Temple, but to hear it, what can He do? Destroy it, the stones are rolling. Then we hear Him, and then we hear it.

Can you hear it?

How do I read a business letter?

What's the difference between a business letter and a love letter? When I read a business letter, I see the words this person writes to me. He ordered 100 Coca Cola bottles. Good.

What do I do when I get a love letter? I read the letter on the level of seeing, and I can also hear the words the way the person utters them when he wrote them. I wasn't there when he wrote the letter, and he didn't even speak out loud when he did. That is only on the level of seeing.

On the level of hearing, I can hear every word they uttered.

When you think about it, this is *Torah sheba'al peh*, the Oral Law, in its deepest depths.

Torah shebichsav, the Written Law, is on the level of seeing. You see the letters, you look at the letters, you understand.

Torah sheba'al peh is not what I see, but what I hear in those letters. Actually, *Torah sheba'al peh* is the utmost combination of seeing and hearing. I look at the letters, and you know what they are telling me? *Gevalt*, what I hear.

The *Torah sheba'al peh* is not about information. That's not what *Torah sheba'al peh* is all about. It is about hearing G-d. When you cry, for one second you close your eyes before the tears come out. What's the holiness of that?

When you close your eyes you don't see, you hear.

When we say the *Shema*, we close our eyes so that we can really hear.

When you go to the mikvah, you are under the water. Your eyes are closed. You don't see anything. *Gevalt*, though, do you hear.

The Tree of Knowledge is that I 'see', just like Chava though that seeing that the apple was good is a good thing 'Vateire Hai'sha'. The Tree of knowledge thinks that its a very special thing to be able to 'see' something and know if it is good or if it is bad. The Tree of life is all about hearing.

When a baby comes into the world it begins crying, begging this world "Please, learn how to hear."

Now when you learn from someone, sure you have to see. When I love someone I want to look at them. But what happens to me inside while I'm looking at them, suddenly I'm hearing so much more than what I see.

Reb Nachman says that it's possible to yell so loud that no one can hear it.[65] But you know who hears it?

Someone who loves you very much. They are not hearing it with their ears — that doesn't work for anyone else — rather, they are hearing it with their hearts.

Some people think that on Tisha b'Av you should be yelling Eichah out like mad. I've seen by a lot of Rebbes that if someone read Eichah with more than a soft voice, they couldn't stand it.

I was privileged to be by the old Vizhnitzer in St. Moritz. I had seen him on Shabbos, but I decided that, one time, I've got to see a Rebbe crying. What is going on by Tisha b'Av? Sadly enough, I couldn't be by the Friediker for Tisha b'Av cause no one was let in.

So listen to this way out thing. I arrive in Switzerland on Friday morning, suddenly I see a *Yiddele* with a *shtreimel*. I asked him where

---

65 *Sichos Haran* 16

he is going, he says to me that the Vizhnitzer was in St. Moritz. Tisha b'Av was Sunday night. So there was a *Yiddele* there started singing Eichah, screaming out Eichah. The Rebbe waves his hand, and starts saying *"Shtiler hait,"* keep quiet. So the *Yiddele* started crying *"Eichah yashvah badad."* After about ten *pesukim* he started yelling again. The Vizhnitzer stopped him and says "No, no." Finally, after the first *kapitel*, someone else took over.

If you can yell loud when you are in pain, it's still on the level of seeing. If it reached so much that nobody can hear it, it reached the level of hearing.

When Mashiach is coming it says *"Ubashofar gadol yitaka, v'kol d'mamah dakah yishama."*[66] "And with a great shofar he will blow, and a still, thin sound will be heard." You will barely hear the sound of the great shofar because Mashiach is so loud, it goes *mamesh* from one corner of time and space till the other.

Where does hatred come from? I look at you, but I don't really see you. The eyes see, but that isn't enough.

The Beis Hamikdash was destroyed because we only saw. With my eyes, I see that you don't keep Shabbos, I see you are evil. I see you are talking evil words. If I could only hear your *neshamah*, if I would hear that voice inside of you which no one can hear, *gevalt* would I love you. There would be no room for hatred.

Mount Sinai is *"Ata horeisah lada'as,"*[67] on Mount Sinai you see everything. Yerushalayim is on the level of hearing.

Ya'akov Avinu was given the Holy Land in the dream. Dreaming is when you see what you hear during the day. So Ya'akov Avinu was given the Holy Land on the highest level of seeing and hearing. Avraham, Yitzchak and Ya'akov — they are on the level of hearing. Not seeing.

"Ve'hayu einecha ro'os es morecha" — "And your eyes shall see your teacher."[68] A Rebbe is about seeing, but a father and a mother are on

---

66   Musaf High Holidays Prayer
67   Devarim 4:35
68   Yishayahu 30:20

the level of hearing. Why didn't Moshe Rabbeinu come into the Holy Land? Now it becomes very clear. Moshe Rabbeinu's Torah is seeing, but the Holy Land is on the level of hearing, so this is not Moshe Rabbeinu. He waits for Mashiach to come when the hearing and the seeing will meet.

Rachel is bringing back Yidden because she is crying so much. Crying is on the level of hearing — "*Kol barama nishma*"[69]— "A voice is heard on high."

Seeing and hearing are separate things, but Mashiach ben David is coming and they are *mamesh* one. The children of Rachel are still on the level of hearing. Mashiach ben Yosef brings us back to hearing. Moshe Rabbeinu brings back the seeing. Then comes Mashiach, "*Bayom hahu yihiye Hashem echad u'shmo echad*," "On that day G-d will be One and His Name will be One."[70]

In the time of the Holy Temple, we were so close to G-d, everything was on the level of seeing. In exile we are so far, it's only on the level of hearing. But when Mashiach comes, the holiness is that it will be both. We will be so close that it will be hearing and seeing together.

Our holy Rabbis teach us that the Holy Temple was destroyed because we didn't love each other. They learned Torah, they kept mitzvos… but it wasn't enough.

Strange, you can do everything right, *mamesh* everything right, but if there are a few people that I can't stand — the Temple is gone.

Oy vey, oy vey, oy vey.

What's the Holy Temple all about? On the street, I don't mind meeting people I don't like. Okay, I meet them and it's over.

In my house, I can only stand people who I love.

Where does it start? We don't know how to look at each other. To

---

69 Yirmiyahu 3:14
70 Zecharya 14:9

look at a human being, especially to look at a Yid, takes more than just good eyeglasses.

Moshe Rabbeinu had clear prophecy. The clearest. When Moshe Rabbeinu asks G-d, "Let me see the land" — what was he asking for?

Doesn't a prophet see from one corner of the world to the other?

The same question can also be asked about when G-d says to Abraham "Go to the land which I will show you." He has to go to the land to see it?

Avraham Avinu has good eyes, he can sit in Charan and see exactly where Ben Yehuda is, he can see Dizengoff, he can see the Holy Wall.

The answer is that there is something deeper than seeing, even deeper than prophetic seeing to see the Holy Land.

G-d has to show it to you. When G-d shows you something, it is much deeper.

❧

What was the greatest gift that G-d ever gave to us?

Shabbos. That was the greatest gift. The bliss of knowing that everything is good. Everything is going to be fine. Everything is already fine.

During the week, we get shortsighted, and we know so little. We worry about everything. During the week, we don't even know how to look at each other.

On Shabbos, G-d gives me new eyes. It says, *"Re'u ki Hashem nason lachem haShabbos,"* — "Look here, G-d gives us the Shabbos."[71]

On Shabbos, we have different eyes. We love each other so much on Shabbos. We understand so much on Shabbos. On Shabbos, we see with G-d's eyes.

Now open your hearts wide:

Whatever Shabbos is in time, Yerushalayim is in space.

When you come to the Holy Wall in Yerushalayim, it's like Shabbos. The Holy Wall gives us new eyes.

---

71 Shemos 16:29

> ❧

Everyone thinks that the *Zohar HaKadosh* is deeper than the Gemara.

In the Gemara, it says "*Ta shma.*"

The *Zohar Hakadosh* says "*Ta chazi.*"

It's true the *Zohar HaKadosh* has "*Ta chazi*" "come and see," but "*Ta shma*" — "come and hear" — is even deeper. I don't see it yet, but I hear it. I know it: "*Mah navu al heharim raglei mevaser,*" — "How beautiful on the mountains are the feet who bring good news."[72]

Do you know what we hear today?

We hear the footsteps of thousands of Yidden coming back to Eretz Yisrael and thousands of people coming back to Yiddishkeit. Thousands and thousands of footsteps.

We should get from "*Ta shma*" to "*Ta chazi*" — to really, really see it.

> ❧

Every day, we say in our prayers, "*Shema Yisrael…*"

If you know Hebrew, you know that *shema* means to hear – "Hear O Israel."

But the *Zohar HaKadosh* says that the word "*shema*" the Hebrew letters *shin, mem, ayin,* stands for "*Se'u marom eineichem*" — "Lift up your eyes high."[73]

So *shema* means both hearing and seeing, because if you only hear but you don't see you can be thrown off.

You have to hear something so deeply that you *mamesh* start to see it.

Let's be real. I don't notice most things — meaning I don't see them — until someone points them out.

That means that seeing actually begins with hearing.

---

72 Yishayahu 52:7
73 *Tikunei Zohar* 49, page 85

Some people come to Yerushalayim, the Holy City, and don't see anything.

And some people come to Yerushalayim and see everything.

It depends who took them to Jerusalem. What explanations did they hear while they were looking at the Holy Wall?

Did they go with some kind of expert travel guide who told them exactly when the Wall was built, exactly when this corner was built, and so on? If so, they didn't actually see the Kotel at all.

Hopefully, they went with a different kind of guide who told them: Do you know what the Holy Wall really is? It was part of the Beis Hamikdash. It held up the Beis Hamikdash!

And then, only then do people begin to *mamesh* see it.

So *Shema* is "*Se'u marom eineichem*" — Lift your eyes up high.

Some people have a tendency to always look down. They look down at others. They look down at themselves, and they even look down at G-d.

Being enslaved to this world means that your eyes are always down. You always look down on everything — down on the world, on Yiddishkeit, even down on yourself — and everyone looks down on you. Everything is down. Some people have this ability to make you look down on everything. These are the people who are enslaved to this world. They are slave people.

But *marom* means very high. "*Shamayim*" is heaven, but *marom* means connecting to *kabbalas ohl malchus Shamayim* — Receiving upon yourself the Yoke of Heaven. This is much higher than just heaven itself.

There are people who are *mamesh* only servants of G-d. They look up to G-d. They look up to you — and make you feel like they are looking up to you. They look up to their *neshamahs*. They make your eyes always look up high.

It's a different kind of looking, with different kind of eyes.

These are G-d's eyes. These are the eyes of Shabbos. These are the eyes of Yerushalayim.

8
What I Learn on Tisha b'Av

We are supposed to love every Jew. Really, we should love the whole world, but let's limit ourselves to Jews for a few minutes.

We are supposed to love every Jew, and people give big speeches about the importance of loving each other. Unfortunately, while they are talking about love, at the same time they are thinking, *I see this guy in the audience. He is a thief, he's mamesh disgusting. Wow, I wish he hadn't come.*

What is going on? The answer is very simple. These people's idea of loving Jews is on the level of the Tree of Knowledge. When you love someone on the level of knowledge, you can cut them into pieces. You can kill them. The Holy Temple was destroyed because we didn't love each other. Were the Jews of that time short on knowledge of how to love other Jews? There was no shortage of knowledge, but it wasn't on the right level.

Do you know what G-d is doing to us on Tisha b'Av? G-d is taking all the Torah we have in our heads, and He is *mamesh* putting it into our insides, into our *kishkes*, into our toenails. But this process hurts so much... *gevalt* does it hurt.

There are two ways of teaching a person not to hurt somebody else's feelings. I can walk up to you and tell you, "Don't do anything that will hurt another person." If you are on the level of Tree of Life, it gets right into you. All I have to do is say, "Don't hurt someone else's feelings," and right away you understand it in the deepest depths.

However, if you are on the level of the Tree of Knowledge, that won't work. It'll stay too intellectual. It won't open your heart. If you are like this, I have to teach you in a different way. I have to reveal to you the depths of what you did when you hurt another person's feelings. *Gevalt*, if you could only see the face of his soul, the tears of his heart. If you only knew what you have done ...

Sometimes, you hurt somebody else's feelings. So you go to this person and say, "Please forgive me." It's all very beautiful, but it's not really so deep. It means you don't really know what you did to the other person. You think it's like a Coca Cola deal: You gave someone pain, and he gives you back forgiveness. It's a business deal — okay, maybe not a pleasant one, but still you are exchanging things.

If you would really know the depths of hurting people's feelings, you wouldn't say a single word. You would just walk up to them and kiss them. What words could possibly be appropriate? How could you ask for forgiveness after what you've done? You don't dare ask....

I learned something about this from my baby. I was doing something, and by mistake I hit her over the head. It wasn't a hard hit, but, *nebech*, she thought that I hit her on purpose.

Right away, I realized one thing. Saying "I'm sorry," wouldn't do any good. She didn't want to hear "forgive me" at that moment — she didn't even know the words yet. Anyway, it wasn't a question of forgiving, because my baby was thinking: *My daddy hit me. Why did he do that? This is the end of the world.*

Instead of saying something, anything, I picked her up and kissed her so much. She was crying, and I was crying and telling her how much I love her. It was so deep — beyond forgiveness....

This is the difference between Yom Kippur and Tisha b'Av.

On Yom Kippur, we ask for forgiveness, and G-d *mamesh* forgives us. We are washed clean. So Mashiach should come one minute after

Yom Kippur is over. Why doesn't he come? What is holding him back? And why does He comes on Tisha b'Av, when we are not even doing *teshuvah*?

On Yom Kippur, I say, "Ribbono Shel Olam, I know the Torah says that I have to keep Shabbos, and I didn't keep Shabbos. Please forgive me."

G-d answers, "So you did wrong? Mazel tov. I know you won't do wrong anymore." It's cute and sweet — even more, it's very holy — but Mashiach doesn't come that way.

Do you know what happens on Tisha b'Av? On Tisha b'Av, the Ribbono Shel Olam shows me what I destroyed in my heart when I didn't keep Shabbos.

I don't even try to ask for forgiveness — it's just too awesome.

On Tisha b'Av, we learn everything we did wrong, and G-d *mamesh* shows us the depths of what we did....

All the Chassidish Rebbes ask a tremendously deep question:

When we made the golden calf, we asked for forgiveness and G-d forgave us. End of story.

Compare this to the spies. When the spies came and told us that Eretz Yisrael is no good, we also asked for forgiveness, but we still didn't get into the Holy Land. Instead we were running around in the desert for forty years.

Why didn't G-d forgive us for the spies like He forgave us by the golden calf?

And, even stronger: If G-d really did forgive us for the spies, why didn't He let us into the Land?

I'm sure there are 2,000 answers to these questions. Here is mine:

Eretz Yisrael is on such a level that everything has to be so deep. It wasn't enough for the spies to come back and tell the Yidden that Eretz Yisrael is bad, and for the Yidden to say, "Ribbono Shel Olam, please forgive us." G-d only would answer, "Maybe you are good and sweet. But you are out — you are not on the level to go into the Land."

And this is the thing about the spies. When it comes to Eretz

Yisrael, it has to be so deep. For the revelation on Mount Sinai, you can ask for forgiveness. We made the golden calf and the Ribbono Shel Olam forgave us. Simple as it is.

But Eretz Yisrael is so deep — it has to be deeper than just asking for forgiveness. Now we see why, on Tisha b'Av, we don't do *teshuvah*. Every year, what each one of us does is to sit on the floor and cry, "Ribbono shel Olam, what did I do to the world? What did I do to myself?"

We are not crying only over the destruction of 2,000 years ago. Tisha b'Av is the day on which I cry over my own destruction....

On Yom Kippur, the Ribbono Shel Olam is our Father, but He is also our King. I have to do what the King wants me to do. The whole forgiveness on Yom Kippur is because G-d is both my Father and my King.

On Tisha b'Av, the Ribbono Shel Olam is only my Father. It's not a question of forgiveness, it's so much deeper. It's a question of love.

On Tisha b'Av, I realize how much my Father wants me to be in a good place – and how much G-d Himself wants the Beis Hamikdash to be rebuilt and Mashiach to come.

❧

When the spies came back from the Holy Land and said bad things about Israel, we believed them a little bit.

We did *teshuvah*, but it still took another forty years for us to enter the Land.

Why didn't G-d forgive us? Why did it take so long?

There is a Torah from the Alexander Rebbe which cuts through everything in our lives.

He says that when you do *teshuvah* for certain things and G-d forgives you, it's as if everything is forgotten. But when you go into Eretz Yisrael, it's not a question of whether you did *teshuvah* for your mistakes. When you go into Israel, the question is very simple — are you merchandise for the Holy Land? Are you the right person to do the job?

If a little spy can come and turn you away from Israel, you might be able to do *teshuvah*. You can cry and say "I'm sorry."

But there is something missing.

Imagine I'm going to get married. Then, one day, we meet up and, suddenly, my *kallah* says, "I'm sorry, but I've changed my mind. I can't marry you right now. Maybe things will be different in a few years."

Then she apologizes and wants to get married.

I'd say to her, "I can't marry you — you're not the person I want to marry. I'm not angry with you. But we just can't get together."

Tisha b'Av is not a day of judging if we are good or bad. In honor of Rosh Hashanah and Yom Kippur you can do your little cleaning. You can wash your shirt, polish your shoes, and cut your nails. You need to do this. It is important — and holy.

That is not what Tisha b'Av is about. On Tisha b'Av, the question is if you are merchandise for Yiddishkeit or not. On Tisha b'Av, what we want — and have to do — is to become the right merchandise again for the Holy Land, the right merchandise for the Holy Temple....

On Tisha b'Av, we are not permitted to learn because we are in mourning.

On Simchas Torah, we don't learn because we are dancing all the time. From the deepest depth, the Torah G-d is teaching me on those days is beyond my knowledge, beyond my mind, beyond everything.

On Tisha b'Av, I learn while I'm sitting on the floor.

Simchas Torah is when I'm dancing, getting up from the floor.

Both are the highest teachings.

There is *teshuvah* of Yom Kippur: After learning all the laws, I realize I was wrong, I have *charatah* (regret) and I learn the laws of repentance. The Rambam says to regret it,[74] and I regret it because the Rambam says to regret it!

If I regret something because G-d says I should regret it, it's not real.

If I step on your toenail and I realize according to everything I've been taught that it's very impolite and a very bad sign to step on someone's toenail, I say to you, "I'm really sorry." I have a very good upbringing; you shouldn't step on people's toenails. I'm completely aware of it. I learned it so therefore I regret that I stepped on your toenail.

Maybe this is enough for Yom Kippur, but not for Tisha b'Av.

On Tisha b'Av, I sit on the floor and after realizing how low I feel, I have something deeper than just regret. On Tisha b'Av, I'm not broken because someone tells me to be broken. On Tisha b'Av, I'm broken from the deepest depths.

I want you to know something very deep. Imagine that I love my wife very much. When does she taste the depths of this love? When I say the words "I love you," she gets a taste how much I love her right this minute. When does she get a taste of what is going on inside of me that made me say I love you? When it hurts so much. When I can't speak.

The same thing is true with our connection to G-d. When do we get a taste of G-d's love? On Tisha b'Av, when G-d says He doesn't ever want to see us again... we suddenly feel how much love was there and how much it hurts.

I'm not missing all the words G-d isn't saying, I'm missing that G-d doesn't want to talk to me now, which is deeper than the words.

When you went to the Holy Temple while it was standing, you didn't have to ask "Where is G-d?" — because He was right there.

---

74   *Rambam, Hilchos Teshuvah 1:1*

I want you to know something of utmost depths.

Imagine I love somebody very much, and we always met in a certain place, under a certain tree. And then, G-d forbid, something happened and we're not so close anymore. When I come to that tree, I'm *mamesh* alone. Can you imagine how much I feel the absence of that person? I'm crying, "*Gevalt*, where is the person I love so much?"

And you know, maybe at that moment I'm closer to that person than I was when we were together. Maybe if we were face-to-face — okay, we love each other, we would be happy. But it wouldn't be so deep. Now when I come to that place I'm all alone. *Gevalt* am I connected to the person I love in the deepest depths....

And now imagine how I'd feel if something happened and the person I love suddenly appeared....

You see, the holiness of the Holy Wall is that for years and years, on Tisha b'Av, we couldn't go back to the place where we had met G-d before. Now we have a chance to go back to the same place. So we're saying to the Ribbono Shel Olam, "Okay, we're back at the Kotel. But where are You? We lost the 6 million, we keep on going through so much. So we just want to know, are You still there, G-d? Where are You?"

And this is why Tisha b'Av is so much deeper than Yom Kippur. Yom Kippur is a personal thing. I'm asking G-d, "Why did I sin? Why didn't You prevent me from doing this, from doing that?" On Tisha b'Av, I don't come to G-d as an individual. On Tisha b'Av, I come to G-d in the name of Judaism, in the name of every Jew — in the name of the whole world. And I'm asking, "What's going on, Ribbono Shel Olam? Where are You? *Gevalt*, where are You?"

There are two situations in life.

In one situation, the greatest blessing is if I know what to do.

The other situation is the other way around: the greatest blessing is if I know that I don't know what to do. Because if, G-d forbid, I think that I know what to do, I'm off. I ruined the whole thing.

There's learning Torah and there is prayer.

The Torah teaches me what to do. I do it.

Tefillah is the other way around. I pray when I know that I don't know what to do.

When is the strongest not knowing what to do?

On Yom Kippur we pray a little bit, we know a little bit what to do: "I know that from now on, I should be better. Yesterday I didn't keep Shabbos, I asked for forgiveness and next Shabbos I'll try to be better."

It's good *davening*, but it's still on the level of Torah. Because I know what to do.

Tisha b'Av is all about prayer. What do you do on Tisha b'Av? Nothing, there's nothing I can do. I'm standing here, the Beis Hamikdash is destroyed, we're in exile, what should I do? You want to promise G-d something? Forget it. You promised a thousand times and you didn't do it, be honest.

On the highest level, Tisha b'Av is more honest than Yom Kippur, because on Yom Kippur I promise 2,000 things. But we all know…

On Tisha b'Av, I don't promise anything. I don't know anything. I don't have anything. On Tisha b'Av, there isn't anything. And that is why we are so sad.

There are two holy days on which we don't learn Torah — Tisha b'Av and Simchas Torah. On Tisha b'Av I'm so broken that I can't learn. On Simchas Torah I'm dancing with joy and I promise that I will learn. But on neither day do I actually learn Torah — because both days are deeper than that.

If the person I love the most writes a book, when do I rejoice over what they have done? Before I even know what they wrote! I'm just so glad that the person I love actually wrote a book.

On Simchas Torah, I'm so high with joy that I don't even know what the Torah says. I'm just so glad that G-d wrote it and gave it to us

Yidden. And on Tisha b'Av I'm crying, because the One I love the most wrote the holiest book, and I didn't even look at it.

❧

On Tisha b'Av we are not permitted to learn because we are in mourning. On Simchas Torah we don't learn because we are dancing all the time. On those two days G-d is teaching us the deepest depths of Torah which is beyond my knowledge, beyond my mind, beyond everything.

On Tisha b'Av I receive this deepest Torah from G-d while I'm sitting on the floor. On Simchas Torah I receive it while I'm dancing, when I get up from the floor.

Both are the highest teachings.

❧

The difference between Mount Sinai and Yerushalayim is very simple. When we stood on Mount Sinai, G-d says, "I took you out of Egypt. I took you out." When G-d takes you out, you are *mamesh* out of it.

When you come to Yerushalayim, G-d doesn't take you out of anywhere. You are taking everything with you and you are coming to Yerushalayim. You have to take everything with you.

After the first Beis Hamikdash was destroyed, we made new vessels and we rebuilt the Holy Temple. When Mashiach comes this time, we aren't going to make new vessels, we are coming with our broken vessels.

Sometimes, a person speaks with young people and tells them, "Okay, listen, everything that happened to you so far, all your broken vessels, forget it. You can be good now, but forget the past."

It's very beautiful to restart. It's on the level of the Second Temple, but this is not what our generation is all about. Our generation is all about coming with the brokenness.

Destruction is also a vessel. The wrong that you did is also part of your life. Everything is a vessel.

If you want to be holy, it's in your vessels. On the level of the Holy of Holies, you bring your unclean vessels. Fill them with holiness.

Tisha b'Av is really the preparation for Yom Kippur; because Tisha b'Av is when you take the broken vessels and these broken vessels now become vessels themselves, this is the whole thing of Yom Kippur. It's paving the way for Yom Kippur... say I did this wrong, I did this wrong; on Tisha b'Av I just know that whatever was until now, so far was not right. It means in my own private life also on a general level. If I go on a private individual level then my brokenness doesn't becomes a vessel. But if I look at my vessels and see they are destroyed and I say "I can't go on like this," then the destruction itself is the greatest vessel in the world. You see what it is, this whole thing made me change because of it.

Why do you hate another person?

Because you see something wrong with them.

Imagine if you could love them and help them fix it. To turn brokenness into a vessel for love. On Tisha b'Av when we reach that level, that brokenness becomes a vessel, I look at every person I hated yesterday because he had no vessels because he's broken and this *mamesh* makes me become a vessel for loving somebody more. So on a certain deep level — when vessels break — they have no meaning. But you see what it is? There are vessels which are broken that only become a real vessel once they are broken.

Can you imagine how all the broken people of the world, all the broken vessels are going to build Yerushalayim?

If you ask me, the two holiest days of the year, if I may say so, are Tisha b'Av and Yom Kippur.

Does anything compare to the very last second before Neilah, when we scream *"Shema Yisrael Hashem Elokeinu Hashem Echad,"* at that moment we receive the forgiveness of Yom Kippur? Yom Kippur is when the Ribbono Shel Olam says "I love you so much, I forgive you for everything."

Tisha b'Av is basically when G-d says to us, "I love you so much that I can't forgive you." Why so?

Because the punishment was beyond proportion.

True, we hated each other, but how much did we hate each other? No one took a knife and killed another Yid. It means we weren't so friendly, we didn't say Good Shabbos friendly enough. So because of that, the Holy Temple is destroyed?

The answer is very simple. When you love someone very much and they do something wrong to you, it might be the smallest thing in the world. If a stranger would do it — it wouldn't even register.

But if the person I love the most does it, I say "I never want to know you again." You want to slam the door in their face and never see them again — but you suddenly realize that you can't. You can't walk away.

Everybody knows that at that moment when the Holy Temple was on fire, at that very moment, the *keruvim* were facing each other. All the Rebbes say the same thing. At that moment when the Beis Hamikdash was burning, Mashiach was already on his way.

9 The Third Temple

There is an old Chassidish Yiddish tune that says: "*Master of the world, I know that the Third Temple will not be built with stones; it will be built with tears. So if all You need is just one more tear, please let it be one of mine.*"

I once met a soldier, one of those holy of holiest soldiers who conquered the Holy Wall. And he told me that he had a dream that 2,000 years of exile is just a nightmare: we never left the Holy Land, and the Holy Temple was never destroyed.

And, in this dream, he thought to himself, *Maybe the Levites are still singing in the* Beis Hamikdash. *Maybe all of Israel is still there, dancing in the courtyard of the Holy Temple.*

So he ran out of his house and climbed over hills and mountains until he reached the hills of Jerusalem.

And yes — it was true!

The Holy Temple was still there, all of Israel was still dancing, and the singing of the Levites was sweeter and deeper than Paradise. He couldn't believe it!

And then he woke up.

When G-d builds the Third Temple, we will know that the exile was just a bad dream. All the pain and suffering never really existed. The 6 million never really died. The Holy Temple was always there.

Let it be that tonight — instead of dreaming — we wake up and find the Holy Temple standing.

Let's meet at this place on the hills of Jerusalem where the holy soldier heard the singing of the Levites. Let's meet the whole world on that hill....

※

If you'd like to know who a person really is, there is a very simple way to find out. Ask them what they think about when they eat.

Some people forget the whole world when they eat.

There are also some people, some holy people, who have different thoughts when they eat.

After they eat, they *bentsch* and say "Thank You G-d for feeding me, for sustaining me. Thank You G-d for the Holy Land."

These people have a question, a deep question. These are the kind of people that while they ate, they remembered all the people that are hungry. They remembered all the people that are heartbroken.

They ask the Almighty:

"If it's true, if it's true that You are feeding and sustaining the world, why is the Holy Temple destroyed, why are so many people hungry, why are so many people standing on street corners across the world?

Why are hearts broken, windows broken, doors broken?"

And then these holy people say:

"Almighty, there is only one way. There is only one way to rebuild the whole world:

U'vnei Yerushalayim Ir Hakodesh

Rebuild Jerusalem, the Holy City

Please G-d, rebuild the capital of the world, the capital of everything which is beautiful and holy in the world. And one more thing: "*Bimheirah b'yameinu* — Let us be there, it should happen in our time."

I once heard from someone who heard Rav Kook say the words "*Sheyibaneh* Beis Hamikdash *bimheirah b'yameinu*," — "May the

Temple be rebuilt speedily in our days," on an ordinary Monday morning.

That is all he heard. This person said that this is all he needed to hear. All his life, he couldn't forget the way Rav Kook said those words.

"*Sheyibaneh* Beis Hamikdash *bimheirah b'yameinu.*"

∽

Speaking of Rav Kook:

The Gemara says, "He who mourns Jerusalem will merit seeing it in its joy."[75] Everybody who mourns for Yerushalayim will have the privilege of feeling the joy when it is rebuilt.

Rav Kook asked: Why did the Gemara say such a person will see "the joy" when the Temple is rebuilt?

Why didn't it simply say that he will be privileged to see its rebuilding?

He answered that it's one thing to *see* the actual rebuilding, and another thing to *feel the joy* of the rebuilding.

A lot of people may see Yerushalayim rebuilt, but it might not bring them joy. The joy will be only given to those who were mourning its destruction.

∽

Do you really mourn the destruction of the Beis Hamikdash? Do you *really want* it to be rebuilt?

How many of us really *want* what we want?

It's not enough to want something. We have to *really want* it. A lot of us want to be very holy Yidden, all of us.

Our problem is that we manage without being very holy because we don't *really want* what we want. I want to do many things. I want

---

75 Tractate *Ta'anis* 30b

to learn all day, but I don't because I want to do other things as well. A lot of people want to marry a certain girl. They never propose to her, because they don't *really want* what they want. If not, I'll marry someone else.

Imagine a person who *really wants* what they want... this is a real human being.

Reb Nachman says that to be in exile means that I don't *really want* what I want. My wanting is in exile.

If I want something, why don't I just do it?

Because I don't *really want* what I want. I'm in exile. If I was a real, free human being, then I would *really want* what I want. There's nothing in my way.

If anything can stop me from what I want to do, it's because I didn't *really want* it that much.

Someone came to the sixth Lubavitcher Rebbe and asked "Should I marry a certain girl?" The Rebbe said "If you ask me, it's already a sign you shouldn't." If you really want to marry her, marry her! Why are you asking questions? You think you should marry her but you don't *really want* to. You're looking for an excuse to get out of it, so don't marry her.

If anybody can stop us from something, that means we didn't want it that much.

Imagine that I want something, but I didn't *really want* it. Then it doesn't happen.

Do I cry?

No. I'm sad, I'm disgusted. I go to my psychiatrist and I really feel awful and let down. But I'm not crying.

Now imagine that same thing. I want it, but I don't *really* want it. But then it happens!

Think of it. I want to marry this girl, but I'm not so sure. Somehow, I don't know what happened, without proposing to her, we just got engaged. We got married. Have you ever been to such a wedding?

How much joy is there at that wedding? If there would be no

crying if it didn't happen, there is no joy when it *does* happen. Either way, the whole concept of wanting doesn't really exist.

She wants to marry him, he wants to marry her, but if it doesn't happen, they'll be okay. They might go see the same psychiatrist. They'll find someone else. Move on.

When do I cry? Only when I *really wanted* something so strong and it doesn't happen — *gevalt*, do I cry.

How do I fix my not *really wanting* what I want? By crying over the Temple. Crying over the Temple connects me back to what I *really wanted*.

I *really want* the Holy Temple to be there. And if the Holy Temple isn't there, I'm *really crying*.

To be in mourning over the Holy Temple means that if it's there — I'm completely happy, but if it's not there I'm really, deeply sad.

So what's our problem? Our problem is that even what we want, we don't *really want*. So what we have to fix is to *really want* what we want.

This is exile. To be in exile is that I don't *really want* what I want.

Reb Nachman says the deepest depths.

People who don't *really want* what they want, do they believe that the whole world really exists only because G-d wants it to?

Do they believe that everything is the way G-d wants it to be?

They can't really believe this — even if they wanted to — because their whole wanting is perverted.

They identify G-d's wanting with their own wanting, as if G-d would want things the way someone who is unsure of his true wanting wants things. Without *really wanting*. Without *really caring*.

Their understanding of wanting is perverted. It means G-d doesn't know what He wants.

Let it be clear to us.

G-d *really wants* what He wants. He created the world because He *really wanted* a world.

Now listen to this. It is an incredibly deep teaching.

What do we do on Shabbos? What are we fixing?

Reb Nachman says on Shabbos we're fixing two things. We're fixing what we love and we're fixing what we want. *B'ahavah u'vratzon Shabbos kodshecha.*

Shabbos is the utmost of G-d's wanting. G-d *really wanted* to create the world, otherwise He wouldn't have created the world.

How does it compare to the way G-d wants Shabbos? He wanted Shabbos even more, because Shabbos is the utmost revelation of what G-d wants.

Imagine the way G-d wants to create the world, or the way G-d wants Mashiach to come. It's a completely different wanting.

Compare the way I want to buy a pound of apples and the way I want my child to be well. It's something else.

We get a revelation of G-d's wanting on Shabbos. *B'ahavah u'vratzon*, with love and will.[76]

Do you know why the Holy Temple was destroyed? Because even while it was there, it was like "I wanted it, and it just happened to be there." We didn't *really want* it. It was not on a Shabbos level.

The third Beis Hamikdash will be on that high, Shabbos-wanting level.

We want it for real.

Imagine what kind of fixing this is. It means that everything I do, I *mamesh want* to do — and I do!

I want to learn, I'm learning.

I want to be a *Yiddele*, I'm a *Yiddele*.

I want to be in Yerushalayim, I'm in Yerushalayim.

Reb Nachman says that when we're crying over the Holy Temple, this is the beginning of the fixing: "I *really want* the Beis Hamikdash to be there." And if it isn't there, I just can't stop crying.

---

[76] Silent prayer on Shabbos

In a watch there are a lot of wheels, but there's one wheel, the inside wheel, which turns everything else.

What happens if that inside wheel doesn't work? I can't say, "Listen, who cares? It's the smallest part of the watch. Everything else is working, so why isn't the watch itself working?" If the inner wheel doesn't work, nothing works.

Reb Nachman says that the Holy Temple is the inside wheel of the world. And the fact is that, sadly enough, the Holy Temple was destroyed, which means the whole world is broken.

We can't fix the world unless this inside wheel is working.

The Holy Temple was destroyed twice.

That means that the world has two enemies — there are two kinds of evil that want to destroy the world.

The first time the Holy Temple was destroyed was by Nebuchadnezzar. Nebuchadnezzar was basically an honest person. He admitted it, saying "I'm a racist, I'm a killer." He made it very clear that he was coming to attack all the women and kill all the men. He was open about it. Therefore, this exile lasted only seventy years, because it's not so hard to fix evil which is clear and open. You know what you are dealing with. You know what you need to do.

The Second Holy Temple was destroyed by Rome. The Romans were worse than Nebuchadnezzar. They were less human, more perverted and crazier. But they said that they came in the name of civilization — to bring civilization to the world.

This is worse. The moment evil people put on themselves the paint of something good, we are in trouble. Imagine that someone says to you, "Hey listen, I love you — *gevalt* do I love you. I have a little knife in my hand and it's right on your back, but it's just a formality." That's the worst thing in the world.

Right now we are getting closer to the rebuilding of the Holy Temple.

Still, we can't rebuild it without making sure that these two evils are completely wiped out of the whole world.

We can't rebuild the Beis Hamikdash until these two evils are also wiped out of ourselves.

~

The month of destruction is called Menachem Av. *Menachem* is the Hebrew word for "consolation," so the name of this month means that G-d, our Father in heaven, is begging us, His children, "Please, console Me."

I heard this *gevalt* Torah from my uncle, who was one of the 6 million. He could have gotten away from Germany a thousand times, but he said, "As long as there is one *Yiddele* left in my city of Hamburg, I have to stay." My father would always tell me this Torah which he heard before he left his brother, my uncle. My uncle would say like this:

"*Nachamu Nachamu Ami,*" —[77] "Console, console my People." The Ribbono Shel Olam is begging us, "Please, Yidden, console Me; please, My People, console Me. Please, *mamesh* console Me!"

And my uncle would say that we Yidden answer, "*Menachem Av*" — how do we console our Father? We promise You that this will be the year. This year, we'll come back to You. This year, we'll come back to the Temple. This year...

~

Why did we make a golden calf?

We didn't want G-d. We wanted *a* god. We didn't *really care*. And we don't.

If someone tells me "I like this girl, but listen, there's this other girl around the corner who looks just the same, just nearly the same." "Okay, let it be her."

There was a classic story. It happened in Hungary somewhere.

---

77   Yishayahu 40:1

This man was engaged to a younger daughter, but then, like Lavan, the same story: The father of the bride got cold feet. "What's going on here, the younger daughter marries before the older?"

So he decided to put the veil over the older daughter. He took his older daughter, put the veil over her, and… the older daughter!

So, after the *chuppah*, they wrote to all the great Rabbis to ask if their marriage was valid. You know what happened? The Rabbis needed some information. How did the boy feel about the switch? After the *chuppah*, they asked the groom:

"Aren't you upset? Look what your father-in-law did to you!"

But the response was "Okay, she's also a woman, who cares". So the question was, because he is so stupid, that maybe he really didn't care before the switch, either… he just wanted to marry *a* woman.

It's not enough to want.

We need to *really want* what we want.

And it starts with the Holy Temple.

How much do we *really want* Mashiach to come? How much do we *really want* peace in the world?

It's on this exile level, we want it, but we don't *really want* it.

We need a new revelation, otherwise how could we fix it?

It's an endless thing, an endless circle. I don't *really want* so I don't really get. I'll never get out of it. I need this one revelation.

On Tisha b'Av, it is revealed in such a powerful way. On Tisha b'Av, we can taste the wanting. The *real wanting*.

Reb Chanina Ben Dosa wanted to bring something to the Holy Temple.[78] But you know, sweetest friends, Reb Chanina Ben Dosa was very poor. He didn't have anything to bring. So he took a stone and put a beautiful *tallis* on it, and started walking to the Beis Hamikdash.

---

78 *Medrash Shir Hashirim* 1

Soon, he realized that he couldn't even carry his own stone. It was too heavy. He was so heartbroken.

Do you know what happened? The Master of the World sent angels to carry the stone for him.

Sometimes we have dreams to do so much, sometimes we have dreams to rebuild the Holy Temple. But then we realize that we can't even carry our own little share.

Listen, friends: It's not really a problem. If we *really want* something, there will always be some angels who will help us.

This is the secret of the Third Temple, and here I want to tell you a little story:

The Rebbe Reb Elimelech dreamed that the Third Temple was being rebuilt. And he saw millions of people — or maybe they were angels — running around, working like crazy. So he stopped one of the angels and said, "You are wasting so much time. If you had fewer people who wouldn't fall all over each other, you could be finished so much faster."

The angel laughed at him and said, "You don't understand, Reb Elimelech. G-d wants as many people as possible to have a part in the rebuilding of the Beis Hamikdash...."

You see what it is, G-d wants everyone to want it to happen, not just a few holy people.

The Arizal says that every month was created with a certain letter. The month of Av was created with the letter *tes*, the ninth letter.

The Medrash and the *Zohar HaKadosh* both say that *tes*, the ninth letter, refers to Tisha b'Av. All the great destructions in the world began on Tisha b'Av, on the ninth, *tes*, of Av: *churban* Beis Hamikdash — the destruction of both Temples; the Inquisition, the 6 million. In the war between Germany and Poland, Germany started invading Poland on Tisha b'Av. The First World War began on Tisha b'Av. Everything was on Tisha b'Av — *tes*. So it seems like *tes* is a letter of destruction and tragedy.

But listen to this way-out thing. Whenever a letter is mentioned for the first time in the Torah, this is the headquarters of that letter. The first time the letter *tes* appears in the Torah is in the sentence, "*Vaya'ar Elokim es ha'or ki tov*" — "And G-d saw that the light was good." The Hebrew word for good, *tov*, begins with *tes*. And what light are we talking about? The Medrash says we are talking about the light of Mashiach. So *tes* is also good — *tov* — the light of the Messiah.

What's going on here?

Reb Levi Yitzchak Berditchever says that all the pain of the destruction of the Temple and of the time before the coming of the Mashiach is like the pain of a woman giving birth to a baby.[79] The nine months of a woman's pregnancy before giving birth to a baby is also the letter *tes*, nine, Tisha b'Av, because Tisha b'Av — *tes* — the ninth of Av, is (*mamesh*) the day on which Mashiach will be born.

It is going to happen. It *will* happen.

The only question is when.

◈

If you want something, you need to ask for it.

You can ask anywhere, but there is one place in the world where you can stand before G-d and ask Him to give it to you *right now*.

This is by the Holy Wall. All the gates are open. You can ask for anything if you have enough chutzpah.

This is Yerushalayim.

G-d wants so much for you.

Is there anything you cannot ask from Him, anything in the world?

Many years ago, I was sitting in the Hilton, and saw a *Yiddele* walking around. He was a *nebech*, lonesome and heartbroken, so I started talking to him.

He tells me his story. He was seventy-two years old. He had

---

79   *Kedushas Levi*, Megillas Eichah, Eili Tziyon

a terrible marriage, and just a few years ago, after his children got married, he got divorced.

He came to Israel all alone. From time to time, I bumped into him, still lonesome and broken.

One time, I saw him. By then, he was seventy-six. He was shining from one corner of the world to the other, looking like he is twenty-six. He was so happy!

I asked him what happened. "What happened? I found my soul mate and I got married two weeks ago. Wait, I have to show you my bride."

Okay, so, obviously, his bride is not twenty years old. He comes with his bride, the cutest yenta you ever saw in your life, she is seventy-five. Do you know something friends, do you know how much they love each other? They love each other so much. It was so unbelievable to see.

She told us her story. She was very happily married for thirty-five years. Her husband passed away and she has grown up children. She realized that now that her children are taken care of, no one in the world needs her anymore.

She thought that most probably, she is on her way out, *Sooner or later, I will die.*

She decided to go to Israel, buy a grave, pay for everything, so then she could die peacefully. She arrives in Israel, but decided that before she buys a grave she is going to daven by the Holy Wall. She comes to the Holy Wall and she tells G-d the story.

"Ribbono Shel Olam, Master of the World, I came here basically to buy myself a grave."

But you know that when you stand by the Holy Wall you heart suddenly opens, she says to G-d:

"But, Master of the World, maybe there is still something for me to do in this world, maybe there is still some life left for me. So I am begging You, if You want to give me something, please give it to me *now*. I cannot wait. If I am meant to die, let me die. If You want to send me a reason to live, send it *now*."

She left the Holy Wall and began to walk, but fell. Couldn't walk straight anymore. So she got herself a cane, and got ready to go to the *chevra kaddisha* to buy herself a grave. She tries to get a cab, but with her fall and her foot, it wasn't so easy.

This *nebech* friend of mine comes, sees her having trouble getting a cab, says to her "I will help you"... and the rest is history.

They got married two days later.

He didn't just want. He *really wanted*.

She didn't just ask G-d to help. She asked G-d to help *now*.

At one time, the Holy Sanzer was sitting on a ship going from Vienna to Budapest. He was so deep in thought, he had a big pipe in his mouth smoking but he didn't even feel that the pipe fell into the water.

He arrives in Budapest and asks the Chassidim "Where is my pipe?" So the Chassidim say "Rebbe, about five hours ago it fell in the river."

So he went off the boat, walks up to the water and says "G-d, if You want to give me back this pipe, give it to me right now." He put his hand in the water and took out the pipe.

If you want something, ask for it.

If you *really want* something, ask to get it "right now."

Do you know how much G-d wants to give us? He wants to give us everything.

Why don't we ask?

During the Six Day War, when we came back to Yerushalayim, we could have asked the Ribbono Shel Olam, "Bring Mashiach!"

At that moment, the gates were open. We were so happy to go out and blow the shofar by the Holy Wall. The Wall is wonderful, but it isn't Mashiach. It isn't the Beis Hamikdash. Why didn't we ask for more?

The *Beis Ya'akov* explains.

Imagine that I want to get some money to build a *gevalt beis medrash*, a house of study. Finally, my cousin arranges that I get an interview with one of the Rothschilds. I fly to Paris to meet him.

Rothschild says, "I'm very much impressed with your work. What can I give you?"

And I think to myself, *I don't want to be a pig and take away all his money. What should I say?*

So I decide to just ask for the least of what I need. I don't want to bother him. I say, "You know what, give me $50,000."

So he gives me $50,000.

But he tells my cousin that he was ready to give me 2 million. Too late — I didn't ask.

Are we asking G-d for what we want or are we so used to compromising?

Are we asking G-d for the Beis Hamikdash?

❧

I remember one of the last Torahs that the sixth Lubavitcher Rebbe taught. Later on, we realized that he was *mamesh* telling us his last will. At that moment, we didn't know.

This is what he said: "We are always coming to G-d like beggars. What's a beggar on the street asking for? A quarter, a dollar. If he has *gevalt* chutzpah, he says, give me five dollars."

The Rebbe said, "We are not beggars. We are not homeless people. Why don't you ask G-d for everything?" So he says, "Can you imagine, the son of Rothschild is standing on a street corner, begging for a quarter. Why don't you ask your father for everything?"

The Ribbono Shel Olam wants to give us everything. Why are we so small?

Every year, we are fixing our vessels just a little bit more. Maybe you feel it, maybe you don't. But it is happening. And the closer we get to Mashiach, hopefully, G-d gives us more. Here comes the deepest Torah in the world.

The Ishbitzer says: Not only does G-d *want* to give it to you. Even better: He *gave it to you already*. It's already in my account. It's just lying there. G-d forwarded it to my account in the holy bank.

Why don't I see it? Because I don't really believe it.

All I have to do is ask. Are you asking? Are you asking for the Beis Hamikdash?

∽

Listen to me, my most beautiful friends.
The first Holy Temple was built because of Avraham.
The second was built because of Yitzchak.
Still, they didn't last.
The third Temple will be built because of our holy father Ya'akov — and it can never be destroyed.
Why?

I had a very deep idea. The first two Holy Temples were built because we wanted it so much. We *mamesh wanted* a G-dly revelation, so badly.

The same thing also happens between people. There is a level of closeness where people can't wait until they are together. They are hungry for each other. This is a very deep relationship; you reveal things to each other which you would have never imagined you would reveal to another human being. Why? Because hunger can be satisfied. We want the closeness. We want to satisfy the hunger.

This might be an Avraham Avinu or a Yitzchak Avinu friendship — on the level of the First and Second Temples.

But it's not on the level of Ya'akov. The Third Holy Temple, Ya'akov's, will not be built because of hunger. It will be much deeper than hunger, so much deeper.

After all these years — after the two destructions, after the

Inquisition, after Auschwitz, and after all the Jewish blood spilled in the Holy Land… it has to be something else, so much deeper.

And it is.

In order to reach that place, we have to go through all the stages. There has to be hunger, and then revelation. After the revelation, there is a different hunger… and then the final revelation, the third revelation, that of Ya'akov.

It is so deep that it's not really a revelation, because a revelation means something outside of you. The revelation on the level of Ya'akov isn't outside at all. It is so deep inside of you.

When something comes from so deep, it lasts forever, it's infinite.

Today, when you go sightseeing, they show you that the Old City is a little city between the walls, so you think that before we were driven out of Yerushalayim, it was a little village.

But the crazy thing was that before the destruction of the Temple, the land expanded. The Land of Israel expanded.

The Holy City expanded. Yerushalayim had 400 schools for children, and every school had 400 teachers, and every teacher had 400 students.

The Holy Temple also expanded. When you come up to the Holy Wall and you have an image of how big the Holy Temple was, it looks like a sweet little house'le. The truth is, when we were *mamesh* there in the Beis Hamikdash, it was a miracle the way we were standing there.

The Beis Hamikdash was "*Miut hamachzik es hamerubah,*" — "The little that could hold the many." Not just Jews came. In the time of the Holy Temple, either you were a pagan or you believed in G-d. The only place where someone who believed in G-d could worship was the Holy Temple.

Do you know how many people came to the Holy Temple? Millions of non-Jews came. In this little place, 40 million people were standing, 40 million.

How could it be?

The Mishnah says *"Omdim tzifufim u'mishtachavim revachim,"* — "They stood crowded and bowed down spaciously."⁸⁰ When you stand you stand, you take up as much space as your feet, but when you have to bow down, you need more space than that. The miracle was that when they bowed down, no one was pushing the other. On Yom Tov, you bow down a little bit. On Yom Kippur, you *mamesh* fall down to the ground.

Something else: On Yom Kippur, you *mamesh* confess everything you did wrong. If you lay one on top of the other, you can hear what the other was saying. But the holiness of the Holy Temple was so holy, that no one heard what the other person was saying. There was *mamesh* three feet between one person and the other, and then around you was another three feet where no one heard the other whispering to G-d.

The Holy Land expanded.

The Holy City expanded.

The Holy Temple expanded.

There was room for anyone who wanted to be there.

There was room for everyone.

Today, also, the more we are getting closer to the coming of Mashiach, the land is expanding, *mamesh* expanding. It is getting ready for us. In the Beis Hamikdash, there will be room for everyone.

There already is room for everyone.

Lets put it this way, when Mashiach is coming, *"Ki beisi beis tefillah yikare l'chol ha'amim."*⁸¹ The whole living world, billions of people will come to Yerushalayim to the Beis Hamikdash and they will fall down before G-d.

It will *mamesh* be the same size... why not?

Can you think of a better way?

---

80   *Avos* 5:5
81   Yishayahu 56:7

It is there for us. Yerushalayim is waiting for us.

How do we get there?

There is a long highway in this world, a long highway. The world is walking for thousands of years. The whole world is looking for a signpost that says Yerushalayim, Yerushalayim, Yerushalayim.

On this earth, on a highway you put up a sign and it says Chicago, New York, Dallas.

The way G-d in heaven puts a signpost, He puts Yidden there, He puts a little Yid there. He puts a little Jewish house, puts a little couple. We bless you that you should just stand on that highway and everybody who sees you will say "Ah, this is the way to Yerushalayim."

We are the way to Yerushalayim. *We* are the signposts.

At a wedding, when we say the seven blessings we don't yell out mazel tov. When you break the glass, you yell out mazel tov.

But what's going on here?

Especially if the broken glass reminds us of the destruction of the Temple, we should be a little bit sad. Why are we yelling mazel tov?

Everyone wants to build Yerushalayim.

You know what the groom and bride are promising each other?

"I swear to you, you and I, we will rebuild Yerushalayim. We will step on every obstacle in the world, we will break through all the glass in the world, but we will get to Yerushalayim."

In their deepest hearts, that is what they are saying.

There are a lot of obstacles to bring up children to be *mamesh emmese* Yidden, but when you swear to each other, nothing in the world can stop you.

There are so many obstacles between husband and wife, sometimes so many wars, so many borders. But if you *mamesh* swear to each other, you will break all the borders, you will break all the laws to be close to each other.

You will get to Yerushalayim.

It is waiting for you. It is waiting for all of us.

※

G-d is waiting for us. He is waiting for each of us. To come to Him alone, and to come to Him together.

Think about it. Everybody says that G-d is One, and they mean that there is only one G-d.

True.

But it means so much more, because if we believe in one G-d then we love the whole world... the whole world becomes one. So I bless you and me and the whole world that one morning very soon, we should all wake up and above the windows of our eyes we will see that the whole world is one.

The world is full of lonely people. Our holy Rabbis teach us that the lonely person is like a little island, an island far from the ocean. Nobody knows where he is.

One day, all the lonely people of the world will come to Yerushalayim. Today, people are lonely only for one person. I miss one person. One day, we will miss the whole world. We will be lonely for the whole word.

One day it will be clear to us that we all are brothers and sisters.

On that day, the Temple will be rebuilt.

On that day, we'll all be back in Yerushalayim.

※

Do you know what's so special about the Jewish People, what is so holy about us little *Yiddelach*?

We have such a good memory. We have such an awesome memory. We never forget Yerushalayim... never.

The Soul of Jerusalem

There is a passage in the Psalms where it says "*Im eshkachech Yerushalayim tishkach yemini*";[82] there is no pain in the world which can make me forget Yerushalayim. "*Im lo a'aleh es Yerushalayim al rosh simchasi*"; there is no joy in the world which can make me forget Yerushalayim.

Our Holy Master Reb Nachman says that wherever a little *Yiddele* goes, he is on his way to Yerushalayim.

If you would stop a Yid 700 years ago on his way to be being burned in the marketplace in Spain, if you would ask him "Tell me little *Yiddele*, what is the last thing in the world you remember?" He would answer "I'm thinking of Yerushalayim… I'm remembering Yerushalayim."

If you would ask a little *Yiddele* on his way to the gas chamber: "Holy little *Yiddele*, where are you going?" He would answer "I swear to you, I'm on my way to Yerushalayim. There is no other place for me to go to. I'm on my way to Yerushalayim.…"

We're always thinking of Yerushalayim.

We're always dreaming of Yerushalayim.

We're always going to Yerushalayim. Each of us is already on the way.

It's the strangest thing in the world.

When you walk on the streets of Yerushalayim, you know that this is the place where our father Abraham walked with our father Isaac.

When you stand late at night by the Holy Wall, you can meet every one of the 6 million holy Yidden.

When you put your fingers on the stones, you can touch their tears. In fact, you can touch the tears of the whole world because we know that all the prayers of the world are coming to Yerushalayim.

---

82   Tehillim 137:5

Everything of value needs Yerushalayim. To put the world together comes from heaven, and it can only open happen in Yerushalayim, there is no other place. Do you think peace comes from Rome, Berlin, Washington, Moscow?

What a joke… only from Yerushalayim.

Everything good needs Yerushalayim. Everything good builds Yerushalayim.

It's strange the way G-d is rebuilding.
It took 6 million to build it.
It took 3 million Jews in Russia to pave the highway.
It takes you and I to build it.
It takes the whole world to supply Yerushalayim with prayer.
It takes the whole world to supply Yerushalayim with tears.
And someday we will know… someday we will know that we were not crying, we were only laughing.
Someday, we will know we were only dancing.
Dancing the whole way — the whole way to the Holy Temple.

In the afternoon before Tisha b'Av, you eat as much as you can. In the minutes before sunset, you wash and eat again.

This time you sit on the floor. You just eat a little bit of bread, an egg, and you get some ashes. Dip the egg in the ashes, and you *bentsch*. This last *seudah* is not eaten with other people. Each person is alone in a corner.

We also eat an egg on Seder night, because Pesach night is always the same night as Tisha b'Av.

There are two reasons why we eat eggs.

The Chasam Sofer says that an egg is the only thing you cook and it gets stronger. Like Yidden, the more *tzaros* (trouble) we have, the more our enemies "cook us," the stronger we get. The harder we get.

That's a sweet teaching. It's true.

There is something even deeper. The Ishbitzer says that when you see an egg, you think that's it. Finished product.

You are mistaken, it's not even born yet. First it has to sit in a little chicken, and then the chicken is coming out of the egg.

We think we are done already? We didn't even begin yet. Whatever happened to us so far was only when we are eggs, but what the Ribbono Shel Olam is doing to us in exile is *mamesh* sitting on us, warming us.

We're not finished. This isn't it.

Mashiach is coming and a real chicken will come out. Real *Yiddelach*.

Now we are "egg *Yiddelach*," but when Mashiach is coming we will be "chicken *Yiddelach*."

No wonder Jewish mothers give you chicken soup! It reminds us:

We're going to be healthy chickens.

We're going to be real Yidden.

We're going to be in the Temple in Yerushalayim.

Our Holy Rabbis teach us that the nations of the world will know before we do when Mashiach comes.

On the one hand, that's very beautiful, but on the other hand it's heartbreaking.

Why should the *goyim* know before us *Yiddelach*, a People who have been waiting for the Messiah for thousands of years? How could it be?

I was thinking a little bit like this.

Sometimes, you wait so long for something that, when it really happens, you can't believe it. The world isn't *really waiting* for Mashiach; maybe they're waiting for him a little bit, but not so much. So when the Messiah comes they will know and they will believe it.

We Yidden wait so anxiously for Mashiach that we *mamesh* won't have the vessels to believe it when he really does come. So we need the world to tell us "*Az yomru vagoyim*" — the nations will tell us that the Messiah is *mamesh* here.[83]

This is what it means when the prophet says, "*Dabru al lev Yerushalayim v'kir'u eilehah*" — "Speak to the heart of Jerusalem and call out to her."[84] *Dabru al lev Yerushalayim* — the word *l'daber*, speak, means that I'm close to you so I can talk normally. But *v'kir'u eilehah* — I only call out if someone is far away.

Why would Jerusalem be far?

What usually happens when that which you long for the most actually takes place? You just can't believe it, you can't believe it is actually happening.

When Mashiach comes, Yerushalayim will run away. *Mamesh*. Jerusalem won't be able to believe that the Messiah has arrived. So G-d said to Yishayahu Hanavi, Isaiah the Prophet: "*v'kir'u eilehah*" — If you see Jerusalem running away, yell after her — tell her that it's *mamesh* true, Mashiach is really here.

Brokenness has its place. Destruction has its place. But there are different kinds of destruction.

Destruction for no reason would be unbearable. Destruction for a purpose is bearable. After the Torah tells us that G-d created heaven and earth, the next passage says, "The earth was filled with chaos, and the Spirit of G-d was upon the waters."

The Medrash says that the Spirit of G-d on the waters means that the spirit of Mashiach was upon the tears.[85] Do you know what that means?

G-d promised us that whenever there is destruction, we will always know that the Spirit of G-d is with us. Mamesh Mereachefes Al

---

83 Tehillim 126:2
84 Yishayahu 40:2
85 *Bereishis Rabba* 2:4

Pnei Hayam, the spirit of G-d is hovering over the waters, over our tears. We will always know that what seems like destruction is just a preparation for something else, something good, to happen. This makes the destruction bearable.

Listen to this story:

One of the holiest Bobover Chassidim who made it through the concentration camps was Yehoshua Volf.

While this Yehoshua Volf was in Auschwitz, he was able to hold out because he knew that Mashiach was coming.

But do you know when he broke down and fainted and couldn't bear it anymore? When the American army marched into Auschwitz to give the Yidden their freedom. All Yehoshua Volf could think was, *For this I was in Auschwitz — that the Americans should free me?* To be in Auschwitz for five years and to not be greeted by Mashiach... this he couldn't bear.

Imagine I have a business meeting and I want to sell 1,000 bottles of Coca Cola. I'm standing there waiting for the businessman to come — I wait for 2,000 years. Finally the man comes. Mazel tov — there's nothing to it.

Now imagine I'm waiting for the person I love the most. I'm waiting and waiting, when suddenly I hear her footsteps. I forget all the pain of my waiting. *Gevalt*, this is so deep.

This is the whole thing about the coming of Mashiach. We've been waiting so long — waiting for 2,000 years is such agony.

But when we hear the Messiah's footsteps, on a certain deep level we'll forget the waiting. All the agony will turn to joy.

※

Can you imagine how deep our relationship is with Yerushalayim that we have come back after 2,000 years?

When you walk away from the Holy Wall you may still not keep Shabbos and you may not be able to handle Yom Kippur. So maybe you're not holy yet.

But do you know what you fix by the Holy Wall? Your Holy of Holies.

And do you know why the Holy Temple was destroyed? Because the Yidden hated each other.

What is in your heart? Love? Or hate?

It comes from the heart. We need our heads, but we need our hearts more.

When Mashiach comes, he will turn the whole world on to G-d. Why haven't we done that already? We have the Torah. Isn't it very holy? Yes, but it is not the Holy of Holies.

The Holy of Holies is Yerushalayim. The Holy of Holies is the Holy Temple. This is the heart of everything. When our hearts are full of love, we'll be able to enter the Holy of Holies. We'll be able to turn the whole world onto G-d.

Our need for Yerushalayim comes from the deepest place of our existence.

And we'll get there. Someday, someday soon.

※

Someday there will be a Great Morning. And suddenly we will see the world in a different light. Someday, late at night, we will walk the streets of the world, and we will see our brothers and sisters, all the people we love. And suddenly we will know that we are all longing for the same thing.

Suddenly G-d will open our eyes, and do you know what we will see? We will see deep down into everybody's heart. And we will see just one holy word written in the deepest depths of everybody's soul: Yerushalayim, Jerusalem the Holy City....

I believe that the 6 million didn't walk into the gas chambers — they walked to Yerushalayim. I could swear that, at the moment when they saw the sun for the last time, suddenly all the lights of heaven were revealed to them. Suddenly they saw there was one G-d; suddenly they saw there was one world. Suddenly they knew they were on their way to Yerushalayim.

Why? Because Reb Nachman says: Wherever you are walking, wherever you are driving, wherever you are going — you're on your way to Yerushalayim.

Let me share this with you, friends:

It's a very high level to consciously think of Yerushalayim, all the time. True.

But it is even higher to know what Yerushalayim is all about. We always think Yerushalayim is longing for us to come to her, which is true.

But believe me, if we had deep eyes and holy ears we would know that Yerushalayim so desperately wants to come to us. Maybe right now we are in Los Angeles, in Paris, in Brazil, in exile. Can you hear the Holy Wall crying because it wants so much to be with us?

The Gemara says that someday all the cities of the world will call to Yerushalayim: "City of peace, city of holiness." Someday, all the streets of the world will be holy, and all the houses will be filled with light.

Yerushalayim is waiting for us, it can't wait for us to come.

Neither can we. We can't wait.

May we be blessed to enter the walls of the Holy City.

We should hear the Levites singing.

Our hearts should be one with the heart of the world.

❧

The Gemara says, "*Abaye mesader ma'aracha*" — "Abaye would give over the order of how things were in the Holy Temple."[86] He would say, "This service would come before this one, and this service before that one."

I heard an amazing story in Bobov: One night, hundreds of Chassidim were sitting with the Bobover Rebbe. It was getting late, but nobody wanted to leave.

---

86 Tractate *Yoma* 33a

So the Bobover Rebbe said, "Abaye tells us that, in the Temple, this service came before that one, and that service came before this one. Why doesn't he say that a certain service came *after* another one? Why is it that when we talk about the Holy Temple, we only use the word 'before' but not the word 'after'?"

The Bobover Rebbe answered his own question like this: "Every night in the Holy Temple, none of the Yidden ever wanted to leave, much like you don't want to leave tonight. But they knew they had to go home, because the next morning would be another day. And it became clear to them that whatever they were doing that night in the Temple was only a preparation for what they would be doing the next day. Today is only for tomorrow, and tomorrow is only for the day after.

"And this is why we only use the word 'before' about the services in the Beis Hamikdash — because each service was only a preparation for the service that would follow…"

When it comes to purifying ourselves, sometimes we think that we have already reached the highest. But everything we've done is only a preparation for something more.

Until the great day comes, everything is just preparation.

The holiest thing about human beings is that we are created in G-d's image and we have choice. Each time I choose something, maybe I'm doing the wrong thing, but I am using my free choice.

So many people are hungry for slavery because it's frightening to have free choice. For certain people, religion is really like a way back to slavery — I don't have to choose. I get myself a little book, G-d's Yellow Pages, and every morning I look up what I am supposed to do and if I don't know the page, I'll pray like mad, "G-d, show me the page," and I tune in and I hear G-d's voice. Clearly, this isn't what God's religion is all about, but what some people do to religion.

On the one hand, I have to know that if I choose wrong, I really lose. It's very important to know the responsibility of choosing. If a person doesn't feel the responsibility of choosing, then they are not human beings.

And, yet, here I want to share with you the deepest depths.

Do you know what it means to really love somebody? To really love somebody means that it's beyond choice. Even if you make every wrong choice in your whole life, I still love you the same. Love is beyond choice.

A house, also, is a place where my being has nothing to do with choice. It is deeper than choice. Do you know where I feel at home? In a place which has nothing to do with choice. Imagine a place where I always have to make excuses why I do this, why I do that. You don't like it anymore because you feel like you are on the street. That means that a house is a place where, even if I choose everything wrong, the door is still open. Anything that has to do with choice is on the street; my house is deeper than choice.

In the Holy Temple, a person comes and stands before G-d and says to G-d, "You know, I made the wrong choice." Aharon HaKohen, the High Priest, comes and says, "You know what? It's okay, you're still okay."

Moshe Rabbeinu is the one who taught us the awesomeness of choice. The Holiness of what took place on Mount Sinai is the awesomeness of choice. Mount Sinai is holy, so holy, but will not turn on the world to G-d because not everybody wants the awesomeness of free choice.

Yerushalayim, the Holy City, the City of G-d is the place where even if you choose wrong — G-d still loves you. Who is the king of Yerushalayim? King David. He made some mistakes. Big ones — but he's still the king.

Eventually, the world will realize that even with all our bad choices, we're still okay with G-d. Some day, the Holy Temple will be a house of prayer for the whole world. It'll be a house, a real house.

Yerushalayim, the Holy City, the City of G-d is the place where even if you chose wrong — it'll be okay.

It already is.

A *Yiddele* came to the holy Sanzer and he said "I'm leaving for Yerushalayim, for the Holy City."

Everybody knows that the holy Sanzer was limping and the greatest thing the Sanzer would do is walk someone to the door. He would very seldom, almost never, walk behind them on the street. This time, "Oh, you're going to Yerushalayim? I'll walk with you."

So they came out to the street and the Sanzer says "You go fast, you can walk. I'll walk behind you slowly till I get there."

Can you imagine the holy Sanzer is walking behind this holy beggar on his way to Yerushalayim?

The holy Sanzer, limping and tears rolling down his holy face, and the whole time he was yelling at the top of his lungs: "Give my regards to Yerushalayim the Holy City!"

He was yelling so loud, "Send my regards to Yerushalayim, the Holy City."

✦

It didn't just happen once. One of his legs was a little paralyzed — just walking to the door showed a great honor to the person visiting him. But if someone would go to the Holy City, Yerushalayim, the holy Sanzer would walk behind him. He would walk and walk and walk until he couldn't see him. And he would call after him:

"Give my regards to the Holy City! Tell the Holy City, that I, Chaim the son of Feige from Sanz, miss Yerushalayim so much. Tell the Holy City that I, Chaim of Sanz, am longing and crying every second to pray in the Holy City. Don't forget to tell Yerushalayim, the Holy City, that I, Chaim of Sanz, am limping on one foot. I know I can hardly walk, but tell Yerushalayim that I am coming."

Let's give our regards to the Holy City, all of us. The whole world is limping. Tell Yerushalayim that we are coming, we are all coming!

Appendix of Historical Personalities

Ba'al Shem Tov (R. Yisrael ben Eliezer): 1698–1760
Maharal (R. Yehuda Loew ben Bezalel): 1520–1609
Mei Hashiloach — Ishbitzer (R. Mordechai Yosef Lainer): 1801–1854
Beis Ya'akov — Ishbitzer (R. Ya'akov Lainer): d. 1878
Noam Elimelech (R. Elimelech of Lizhensk): 1717–1787
Radomsker Rebbe (R. Shlomo Rabinowitz): 1801–1866
Reb Tzadok HaKohen Rabinowitz of Lublin: 1823–1901
Reb Nachman of Breslov: 1772–1810
Sanzer Rebbe (R. Chaim Halberstam): 1793–1876
Vorker Rebbe (R. Yitzchak of Vorke): 1779–1848
Reb Levi Yitzchak of Berditchev – 1740–1809
Chasam Sofer (R. Moshe Schreiber): 1762–1839
Arizal (R. Yitzchak Luria): 1534–1572
R' Avraham Yitzchak HaKohen Kook: 1865–1935
Kozhnitzer Maggid (R. Yisrael Hopstein): 1737–1814
Reb Tzvi Hersh of Riminov: 1778–1847
Reb Shmelke of Nikolsburg: 1726–1778
Chozeh (Seer) of Lublin (R' Ya'akov Yitzchak Horowitz): 1745–1815
Reb Ahron Karliner: 1802–1872
Reb Nosson Steinhartz of Breslov: 1780–1844

Appendix of Historical Personalities

Alter Rebbe (R. Shneur Zalman of Liadi): 1745–1812
Reb Avraham HaMalach (the angel): 1739–1776
Reb Elizer Horowitz of Dzhikov: d. 1860
Reb Shimon Elbaum of Yaroslov: 1759–1850
Reb Yechezel Shraga Halbershtam of Shinov: 1813–1898
Reb Dovid of Lelov: 1746–1814
R' Shlomo Molcho: 1500–1532
Reb Ben Zion Halberstam of Bobov: 1874–1941
The Pshischer – Reb Simcha Bunim Bonhart: 1765–1827
Reb Chaim Meir Hager of Vizhnitz: 1881–1972

About Rabbi Shlomo Carlebach

Rabbi Shlomo Carlebach was born in Berlin, Germany in 1925. He grew up with his twin brother, Eli Chaim, and his sister, Shulamith, in a town near Vienna where his father, Rabbi Naftali, was the Chief Rabbi. In 1939, as World War II began to escalate and the Nazis' grip tightened, Shlomo and his family miraculously escaped to New York where he spent time learning by some of the greatest Torah scholars of the last century, such as Rabbi Aharon Kotler, Rabbi Shlomo Heiman, and the Lubavitcher Rebbe. He was known as being brilliant.

Even as a young boy, Shlomo's vision and clarity of thought always set him apart from his peers.

Through that vision, courage, and a deep love of all people, Shlomo took on a mission and set off on a path that many didn't believe in. Reb Shlomo believed that his raison d'être (reason for existing) was to uplift, inspire, and bring joy to every human being.

Indeed, through his words of Torah, music, and stories, Reb Shlomo touched the hearts and souls of all who were blessed to hear him. He sought to remind people that they are never alone, that there is one G-d who loves them, and that every person has a unique and important mission to discover for themselves. He was able to mend the spirits and lives of the most broken and distraught people worldwide — people of all faiths and cultures. Much of Reb Shlomo's life was spent traveling the world, where he would sing with the poor, the lost, and the lonely, and always explain that it was *he* who learned from *them*.

Even now, since his passing in 1994, hundreds of thousands of lives have been, and continue to be, changed by Reb Shlomo's teachings, messages, and melodies.

About the Author

Rabbi Shlomo Katz is a world-renowned musician. He has released seven albums and has conducted numerous concert tours throughout the United States, Israel, South Africa, South America, Australia, Asia, and Europe. After learning in Yeshivat HaMivtar in Efrat, Israel, he received his *semichah* — rabbinic ordination — in 2006 and has been teaching ever since. Rabbi Katz has been an integral part of building the Shlomo Carlebach Foundation which has been working to preserve, publish and distribute the legacy of Rabbi Shlomo Carlebach *zt"l* as a Jewish national treasure.

In between his teaching in Efrat, Yeshivat Simchat Shlomo, and Web Yeshiva, Shlomo continues to tour, teach, and perform throughout the world. Rabbi Katz lives in Efrat, with his wife Bina and daughters, Tiferet and Ora Menucha.

www.shlomokatz.com
info@shlomokatz.com

About Mosaica Press

Mosaica Press is an independent publisher of Jewish books. Our authors include some of the most profound, interesting, and entertaining thinkers and writers in the Jewish community today. There is a great demand for high-quality Jewish works dealing with issues of the day — and Mosaica Press is helping fill that need. Our books are available around the world. Please visit us at www.mosaicapress.com or contact us at info@mosaicapress.com. We will be glad to hear from you.